Statistics 2
for AQA

CAMBRIDGE
UNIVERSITY PRESS

The School Mathematics Project

SMP AS/A2 Mathematics writing team John Ling, Paul Scruton, Susan Shilton, Heather West

SMP design and administration Melanie Bull, Pam Keetch, Nicky Lake, Cathy Syred, Ann White

The authors thank Sue Glover for the technical advice she gave when this AS/A2 project began and for her detailed editorial contribution to this book. The authors are also very grateful to those teachers who advised on the book at the planning stage and commented in detail on draft chapters.

CAMBRIDGE UNIVERSITY PRESS
Cambridge, New York, Melbourne, Madrid, Cape Town, Singapore, São Paulo

Cambridge University Press
The Edinburgh Building, Cambridge CB2 2RU, UK

www.cambridge.org
Information on this title: www.cambridge.org/9780521605311

© The School Mathematics Project 2005

First published 2005

Printed in the United Kingdom at the University Press, Cambridge

A catalogue record for this publication is available from the British Library

ISBN-13   978-0-521-60531-1 paperback
ISBN-10   0-521-60531-8 paperback

Typesetting and technical illustrations by The School Mathematics Project

The authors and publisher are grateful to the Assessment and Qualifications Alliance for permission to reproduce questions from past examination papers and the tables on pages 110–115. Individual questions are marked AQA.

Using this book

Each chapter begins with a **summary** of what the student is expected to learn.

The chapter then has sections lettered A, B, C, ... (see the contents overleaf). In most cases a section consists of development material, worked examples and an exercise.

The **development material** interweaves explanation with questions that involve the student in making sense of ideas and techniques. Development questions are labelled according to their section letter (A1, A2, ..., B1, B2, ...) and answers to them are provided.

D Some development questions are particularly suitable for discussion – either by the whole class or by smaller groups – because they have the potential to bring out a key issue or clarify a technique. Such **discussion questions** are marked with a bar, as here.

K **Key points** established in the development material are marked with a bar as here, so the student may readily refer to them during later work or revision. Each chapter's key points are also gathered together in a panel after the last lettered section.

The **worked examples** have been chosen to clarify ideas and techniques, and as models for students to follow in setting out their own work. Guidance for the student is in italic.

The **exercise** at the end of each lettered section is designed to consolidate the skills and understanding acquired earlier in the section. Unlike those in the development material, questions in the exercise are denoted by a number only.

Starred questions are more demanding.

After the lettered sections and the key points panel there may be a set of **mixed questions**, combining ideas from several sections in the chapter; these may also involve topics from earlier chapters.

Every chapter ends with a selection of **questions for self-assessment** ('Test yourself').

Included in the mixed questions and 'Test yourself' are **past AQA exam questions**, to give the student an idea of the style and standard that may be expected, and to build confidence.

Contents

1 Discrete random variables

In this chapter you will learn
- what is meant by the probability distribution of a discrete random variable
- how to find the mean, variance and standard deviation of a discrete random variable and of a function of a discrete random variable

A Probability distribution (answers p 116)

The diagram shows a spinner. The circle is divided into 10 equal sectors. The pointer is equally likely to stop in each sector.

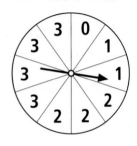

The probabilities of scoring 0, 1, 2, 3 are as shown in this table.

Score	0	1	2	3
Probability	0.1	0.2	0.3	0.4

The score is an example of a **discrete random variable**.

A discrete random variable is a variable that can take individual values (usually integers), each with a given probability.

Let X stand for the score. (Capital letters are used for random variables.)
$P(X = 2)$ means the probability that the score is 2. So $P(X = 2) = 0.3$.

The complete set of probabilities for all the possible values of X is called the **probability distribution** of X.

x	0	1	2	3
$P(X = x)$	0.1	0.2	0.3	0.4

Notice that a lower-case (small) x is used for individual values of the random variable X.

A1 What is the sum of all the probabilities in the table? Complete the following statement.

$\sum P(X = x) = \ldots$

The probability distribution can also be shown as a 'stick graph'. The total of the heights of the sticks is 1.

A2 A board game is played with an ordinary dice.
A player moves 1 square if the dice shows one, two or three, 2 squares if it shows four or five and 3 squares if it shows six.

The random variable X is the number of squares moved. Copy and complete this table of the probability distribution of X.

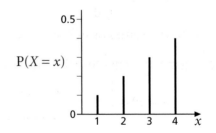

x	1	2	3
$P(X = x)$			

A3 In a game, two ordinary dice are thrown together. The number of squares moved is 0 if both dice show less than four, 2 if both show more than four, and 1 otherwise.

The random variable Y is the number of squares moved.
Make a table showing the values of $P(Y = y)$ for $y = 0$, 1 and 2.

A discrete **uniform** distribution is one where all the probabilities are equal.

An example is the score X from a single throw of an ordinary dice.
The distribution and its stick graph are shown below.

x	1	2	3	4	5	6
$P(X = x)$	$\frac{1}{6}$	$\frac{1}{6}$	$\frac{1}{6}$	$\frac{1}{6}$	$\frac{1}{6}$	$\frac{1}{6}$

This probability distribution can be summarised as

$$P(X = x) = \begin{cases} \frac{1}{6} & x = 1, 2, 3, 4, 5, 6 \\ 0 & \text{otherwise} \end{cases}$$

The '0 otherwise' statement shows that X can only take the values 1, 2, 3, 4, 5, 6.

Specifying a distribution by means of a formula

Some probability distributions may be given as formulae in terms of x.
For example, here is the distribution for scores on the spinner on the opposite page.

$$P(X = x) = \begin{cases} \dfrac{x+1}{10} & x = 0, 1, 2, 3 \\ 0 & \text{otherwise} \end{cases}$$

In this example, $P(X = 0) = \frac{1}{10} = 0.1$, $P(X = 1) = \frac{2}{10} = 0.2$, and so on.
You have already checked, in question A1, that $\sum P(X = x) = 1$ for this distribution.

K If X is any discrete random variable, then $\sum P(X = x) = 1$.

A4 A discrete random variable X has the probability distribution given by
$$P(X = x) = \begin{cases} \dfrac{x+3}{18} & x = 0, 1, 2, 3 \\ 0 & \text{otherwise} \end{cases}$$
Find the values of $P(X = x)$ for $x = 0$, 1, 2, 3 and check that $\sum P(X = x) = 1$.

A5 Explain why the function below cannot be a probability distribution.
$$P(X = x) = \begin{cases} \dfrac{x}{20} & x = 1, 2, 3, 4, 5, 6 \\ 0 & \text{otherwise} \end{cases}$$

A6 It is suggested that the following is the probability distribution of a discrete random variable X.
$$P(X = x) = \begin{cases} \dfrac{4-x}{5} & x = 1, 2, 3, 4, 5 \\ 0 & \text{otherwise} \end{cases}$$
Explain why the function cannot be a probability distribution.

Example 1

A probability distribution is given as $P(X = x) = \begin{cases} kx & x = 1, 2, 3, 4, 5, 6 \\ 0 & \text{otherwise} \end{cases}$

(a) Find the value of k.   (b) Find $P(X \geq 4)$.

Solution

(a) The probability distribution is shown in this table.

x	1	2	3	4	5	6
$P(X = x)$	k	$2k$	$3k$	$4k$	$5k$	$6k$

$\sum P(X = x)$ must be equal to 1.

So $k + 2k + 3k + 4k + 5k + 6k = 1 \implies 21k = 1 \implies k = \frac{1}{21}$

(b) $P(X \geq 4) = P(X = 4, 5 \text{ or } 6) = P(X = 4) + P(X = 5) + P(X = 6)$

$$= \tfrac{4}{21} + \tfrac{5}{21} + \tfrac{6}{21} = \tfrac{15}{21} = \tfrac{5}{7}$$

Exercise A (answers p 116)

1 The probability distribution of a discrete random variable X is defined by

$$P(X = x) = \begin{cases} \frac{1}{15}x & x = 1, 2, 3, 4, 5 \\ 0 & \text{otherwise} \end{cases}$$

Find $P(X = 1)$, $P(X = 2)$, $P(X = 3)$, $P(X = 4)$ and $P(X = 5)$, and show that they add up to 1.

2 A newsagent notices that no customer buys more than four newspapers or magazines and that customers are more likely to buy two or three than one or four.

A student suggests that the number bought might be modelled by a discrete random variable X with the following probability distribution.

$$P(X = x) = \begin{cases} \frac{1}{20}x(5 - x) & x = 1, 2, 3, 4 \\ 0 & \text{otherwise} \end{cases}$$

Find the values of $P(X = x)$ and draw a stick graph of this distribution.

3 The number of flowers on plants of a certain species is modelled as a discrete random variable X with the probability distribution $P(X = x)$ as defined below.

$$P(X = x) = \begin{cases} kx^2 & x = 1, 2, 3, 4 \\ 0 & \text{otherwise} \end{cases}$$

(a) Write down, in terms of k, the values of $P(X = 1)$, $P(X = 2)$, $P(X = 3)$ and $P(X = 4)$.

(b) Find the value of k.   (c) Find $P(X \geq 3)$.

4 The probability distribution of a discrete random variable X is given by

$$P(X = x) = \begin{cases} k(4 - x) & x = 1, 2, 3 \\ k(x - 3) & x = 4 \\ 0 & \text{otherwise} \end{cases}$$

Find the value of k.

B Mean or expected value (answers p 116)

B1 Here are two spinners. You are invited to choose a spinner and spin it. You will win the amount the arrow points to.

Which spinner would you choose, and why?

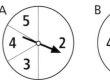

B2 Which of these two spinners would you choose, and why?

When you decide which spinner is 'better', you need to take account of both the scores and their probabilities. A high score with a very low probability is no better than a low score with a high probability.

Here is the probability distribution of the score on spinner C.

Score	2	3	4	5
Probability	$\frac{1}{3}$	$\frac{1}{6}$	$\frac{1}{3}$	$\frac{1}{6}$

One way to think about the problem is to imagine that the spinner is spun a large number of times.

For example, for spinner C the probability of a score of 2 is $\frac{1}{3}$. If the spinner is spun 60 times, then you would expect to get a score of 2 about 20 times.

The expected frequencies of the possible scores if there are 60 spins are shown in this table.

Score	2	3	4	5
Probability	20	10	20	10

These frequencies can be used to calculate a mean score:

$$\text{Mean score} = \frac{(2 \times 20) + (3 \times 10) + (4 \times 20) + (5 \times 10)}{60} = \frac{200}{60} = 3\frac{1}{3}$$

It was unnecessary to multiply all the probabilities by 60 and then divide by 60 at the end. The mean score can be calculated using the probabilities themselves.

$$\text{Mean score} = \left(2 \times \tfrac{1}{3}\right) + \left(3 \times \tfrac{1}{6}\right) + \left(4 \times \tfrac{1}{3}\right) + \left(5 \times \tfrac{1}{6}\right) = 3\frac{1}{3}$$

This mean score can be compared with the mean scores for the other spinners, to see which one is better 'on average'.

B3 Find the mean score for each of the spinners A, B and D. Which spinner is 'best'?

The mean value of a random variable X is also called the **expected value** of X, which is written $E(X)$. It is also known as the **expectation** of X.

So if X is the score obtained from spinner C, then $E(X) = 3\frac{1}{3}$.

To calculate $E(X)$, each possible value of the random variable is multiplied by its probability, and the products are added together.

The possible values of X are often denoted by $x_1, x_2, x_3, \ldots$ and the corresponding probabilities by $p_1, p_2, p_3, \ldots$

x	x_1	x_2	x_3	...
$P(X = x)$	p_1	p_2	p_3	...

Using this notation, $E(X) = \sum x_i p_i$.

B4 Find the mean of the random variable X whose probability distribution is shown in this table.

x	0	1	2	3
$P(X = x)$	0.35	0.3	0.2	0.15

Imagine a gambling machine on which you pay £1 to play. Suppose the payout could be zero (with probability 0.7) or £2 (with probability 0.2) or £5 (with probability 0.1).

The payout in pounds X is a discrete random variable with the probability distribution shown in this table.

x	0	2	5
$P(X = x)$	0.7	0.2	0.1

B5 Find the value of $E(X)$.
What does it tell you about the machine? (Remember you pay £1 to play.)

B6 On another machine you pay 50p per game. The payout is £0 (with probability 0.75) or £1 (with probability 0.2) or £10 (with probability 0.05).

Let Y be the payout in pounds on one play of this machine.

(a) Make a table of the probability distribution of Y.

(b) Calculate $E(Y)$.

(c) From the player's point of view, is this machine better or worse than the previous one?

B7 Gemma suggests a dice game to her brother Carl.
Carl is to roll two ordinary dice.

If the two numbers are equal, Gemma will give him 20p.
If they differ by one, she will give him 5p.
If they differ by more than one, he will give Gemma 10p.

The amount that Carl could win could be −10p (10p loss), 5p or 20p.

(a) Work out the probability of each of the three outcomes (as a fraction).
Let X represent Carl's winnings in a single game.
Make a table of the probability distribution for X.

x	−10	5	20
$P(X = x)$			

(b) Find $E(X)$. What does this tell you about the game?

B8 Gemma suggest a different game. Carl is to roll three ordinary dice.

If the three numbers are all even, Gemma will give him 20p.
If the three numbers are all odd, she will give him 50p.
If the numbers are a mixture of odd and even, Carl will give her 10p.

(a) Let Y represent Carl's winnings in this game.
Make a table of the probability distribution for Y.

(b) Find $E(Y)$. What does it tell you about the game?

B9 The table shows the probability distribution of the discrete random variable W. Given that $E(W) = 1.5$, find a and b.

w	0	1	2
$P(W = w)$	0.15	a	b

Example 2

The probability distribution of a discrete random variable X is defined by

$$P(X = x) = \begin{cases} \frac{1}{15}x & x = 1, 2, 3, 4, 5 \\ 0 & \text{otherwise} \end{cases}$$

Find $E(X)$.

Solution

The probability distribution of X is shown here.

x	1	2	3	4	5
$P(X = x)$	$\frac{1}{15}$	$\frac{2}{15}$	$\frac{3}{15}$	$\frac{4}{15}$	$\frac{5}{15}$

$$E(X) = \left(1 \times \tfrac{1}{15}\right) + \left(2 \times \tfrac{2}{15}\right) + \left(3 \times \tfrac{3}{15}\right) + \left(4 \times \tfrac{4}{15}\right) + \left(5 \times \tfrac{5}{15}\right) = \tfrac{55}{15} = 3\tfrac{2}{3}$$

Example 3

The probability function of the discrete random variable X is shown in the table.
Given that $E(X) = 2.95$, find the values of a and b.

x	1	2	3	4
$P(X = x)$	0.2	a	0.25	b

Solution

The total probability must be 1, so $\quad a + b = 0.55 \qquad\qquad (1)$

$E(X) = 2.95$, so $(1 \times 0.2) + 2a + (3 \times 0.25) + 4b = 2.95$

$\qquad\qquad\qquad\qquad \Rightarrow \quad 2a + 4b = 2 \ \text{ or } \ a + 2b = 1 \quad (2)$

By subtracting (1) from (2), $b = 1 - 0.55 = 0.45$, from which $a = 0.55 - 0.45 = 0.1$

Exercise B (answers p 116)

1 The table shows the probability distribution of a discrete random variable X. Find

x	0	1	2	3
$P(X = x)$	0.08	0.15	a	0.35

(a) the value of a (b) $E(X)$

2 The probability distribution of a discrete random variable X is given by

$$P(X = x) = \begin{cases} k(20 - x^2) & x = 1, 2, 3, 4 \\ 0 & \text{otherwise} \end{cases}$$

(a) Find the value of k.   (b) Find $E(X)$.

3 The probability distribution of a discrete random variable Y is shown in the table. Given that $E(Y) = 1.4$, find the value of   (a) β (b) α

y	0	1	2	3
$P(Y = y)$	α	0.3	0.4	β

4 The probability distribution of a discrete random variable W is given by this table.
Given that $E(W) = 2.8$, find the values of α and β.

w	1	2	3	4
$P(W = w)$	α	0.3	0.3	β

5 The random variable U is uniformly distributed over the values $0, 1, 2, 3, \ldots, 9$.
Find $E(U)$.

C Expectation of a function of a discrete random variable (answers p 117)

Suppose a tetrahedral dice has the numbers 1, 2, 3, 4 on its faces. The score X from a single throw of this dice has the probability distribution shown in this table.

Value of X	1	2	3	4
Probability	$\frac{1}{4}$	$\frac{1}{4}$	$\frac{1}{4}$	$\frac{1}{4}$

In a game, this dice is thrown and the score doubled. The 'double score' is a random variable. Call it Y.

Then $Y = 2X$ and the probability distribution of Y is as shown in the second table.
Each value of X is doubled; the probabilities stay the same.

Value of Y	2	4	6	8
Probability	$\frac{1}{4}$	$\frac{1}{4}$	$\frac{1}{4}$	$\frac{1}{4}$

C1 (a) Find the expected value of X.

    (b) Do the same for Y, where $Y = 2X$.

    (c) What is the relationship between $E(Y)$ and $E(X)$?

C2 In a different game with the same dice, 3 is added to the score. This gives the random variable W, where $W = X + 3$.

    (a) Make a table for the probability distribution of W.

    (b) Find $E(W)$.

    (c) How are the expected values of W and X related?

C3 Suppose the dice score is doubled and then 3 is added. This gives the random variable V, where $V = 2X + 3$.

    (a) Copy and complete this table for the probability distribution of V.

Value of V	5			
Probability	$\frac{1}{4}$	$\frac{1}{4}$	$\frac{1}{4}$	$\frac{1}{4}$

    (b) Find $E(V)$.

    (c) What is the relationship between $E(V)$ and $E(X)$?

C4 Suppose the dice score is multiplied by 4 and then 5 is added. This gives the random variable U, where $U = 4X + 5$.

    (a) Without first making a table for the distribution of U, write down what you think is the value of $E(U)$.

    (b) By making a table, check your answer to part (a).

C5 Given that a and b are numbers, what do your results in C1–C4 suggest about the value of $E(aX + b)$?

> **K** If X is a discrete random variable and a and b are numbers, then the random variable $aX + b$ is called a **linear function** of X.
>
> $E(aX + b) = aE(X) + b$

The reason $E(aX + b) = aE(X) + b$ is as follows.

(1) First suppose that each possible value $x_1, x_2, x_3, \ldots$ is multiplied by a.
To find the new mean we have to calculate $ax_1 p_1 + ax_2 p_2 + ax_3 p_3 + \ldots$
$$= a(x_1 p_1 + x_2 p_2 + x_3 p_3 + \ldots)$$
So multiplying every value by a results in the mean being multiplied by a.

(2) Now suppose that every possible value is increased by b.
The new mean is $(x_1 + b)p_1 + (x_2 + b)p_2 + (x_3 + b)p_3 + \ldots$
$$= (x_1 p_1 + x_2 p_2 + x_3 p_3 + \ldots) + b(p_1 + p_2 + p_3 + \ldots)$$
Because $p_1 + p_2 + p_3 + \ldots = 1$, it follows that adding b to each value results in adding b to the mean.

(3) If we both multiply each value by a and then add b, the mean is first multiplied by a and then b is added.
So $E(aX + b) = aE(X) + b$.

C6 W is a discrete random variable for which $E(W) = 2.5$.
Find the value of

(a) $E(5W)$ (b) $E(5W - 2)$ (c) $E(-3W)$ (d) $E(-3W + 1)$ (e) $E(10 - 2W)$

Non-linear functions

Here is the probability distribution of a discrete random variable X.

x	1	2	3	4
$P(X = x)$	0.1	0.3	0.4	0.2

Another discrete random variable Y is defined in terms of X as follows:
$$Y = \frac{12}{X}$$

Y is not of the form $aX + b$, so the simple way of calculating $E(Y)$ from $E(X)$ cannot be used.

Instead, we have to find the probability distribution of Y.

If $X = 1$, then $Y = \frac{12}{1} = 12$.

If $X = 2$, then $Y = \frac{12}{2} = 6$, and so on.

The four possible values of Y, together with the corresponding probabilities, are as shown in this table.

y	12	6	4	3
$P(Y = y)$	0.1	0.3	0.4	0.2

C7 (a) Find $E(Y)$.

(b) Show that, although $Y = \frac{12}{X}$, $E(Y)$ is **not** equal to $\frac{12}{E(X)}$.

One function that is important in applications is the function X^2.

C8 Let X be the score on a throw of an ordinary dice. The probability distribution of X is shown here.

x	1	2	3	4	5	6
$P(X = x)$	$\frac{1}{6}$	$\frac{1}{6}$	$\frac{1}{6}$	$\frac{1}{6}$	$\frac{1}{6}$	$\frac{1}{6}$

Suppose each score is squared. This gives the random variable X^2, whose probability distribution is shown in this table.

x^2	1	4	9	16	25	36
$P(X^2 = x^2)$	$\frac{1}{6}$	$\frac{1}{6}$	$\frac{1}{6}$	$\frac{1}{6}$	$\frac{1}{6}$	$\frac{1}{6}$

(a) Find $E(X^2)$.   **(b)** Find $E(X)$ and show that $E(X^2)$ is not equal to $[E(X)]^2$.

C9 The discrete random variable Y has the probability distribution given in this table.

y	1	2	3	4
$P(Y = y)$	0.1	0.3	0.4	0.2

(a) Find $E(Y^2)$.   **(b)** Show that $E(Y^2) \neq [E(Y)]^2$.

If the possible values of X are $x_1, x_2, x_3, \ldots$,
then the corresponding values of X^2 are $x_1{}^2, x_2{}^2, x_3{}^2, \ldots$
So $E(X^2) = x_1{}^2 p_1 + x_2{}^2 p_2 + x_3{}^2 p_3 + \ldots$
Similarly, $E(X^3) = x_1{}^3 p_1 + x_2{}^3 p_2 + x_3{}^3 p_3 + \ldots$
$$E(X^{-1}) = x_1{}^{-1} p_1 + x_2{}^{-1} p_2 + x_3{}^{-1} p_3 + \ldots$$

The general rule can be stated as follows.

If $g(X)$ is a function of the discrete random variable X, then
$$E[g(X)] = g(x_1)p_1 + g(x_2)p_2 + g(x_3)p_3 + \ldots = \Sigma g(x_i)p_i$$

Two other useful results follow from this expression for $E[g(X)]$.

Expectation of the sum of two functions $f(X) + g(X)$

If $f(X)$ and $g(X)$ are two functions of X, then
$$
\begin{aligned}
E[f(X) + g(X)] &= [f(x_1) + g(x_1)]p_1 + [f(x_2) + g(x_2)]p_2 + \ldots \\
&= [f(x_1)p_1 + f(x_2)p_2 + \ldots] + [g(x_1)p_1 + g(x_2)p_2 + \ldots] \\
&= E[f(X)] + E[g(X)]
\end{aligned}
$$

In words, the expectation of the sum of two functions of X is the sum of the expectations.
For example, $E(X^3 + X^2) = E(X^3) + E(X^2)$.

Expectation of $k\,g(X)$, where k is a number

If $g(X)$ is a function of X, then
$$
\begin{aligned}
E[k g(X)] &= k g(x_1)p_1 + k g(x_2)p_2 + k g(x_3)p_3 + \ldots \\
&= k[g(x_1)p_1 + g(x_2)p_2 + g(x_3)p_3 + \ldots] \\
&= k E[g(X)]
\end{aligned}
$$
For example, $E(3X^2) = 3\,E(X^2)$.

Example 4

The probability distribution of the discrete random variable X is given by

$$P(X = x) = \begin{cases} \frac{1}{30}x & x = 4, 5, 6, 7, 8 \\ 0 & \text{otherwise} \end{cases}$$

Find   (a) $E(X)$ (b) $E(3X - 2)$ (c) $E(10 - X)$

Solution

(a) The probability distribution of X is

x	4	5	6	7	8
$P(X = x)$	$\frac{4}{30}$	$\frac{5}{30}$	$\frac{6}{30}$	$\frac{7}{30}$	$\frac{8}{30}$

$$E(X) = 4 \times \tfrac{4}{30} + 5 \times \tfrac{5}{30} + 6 \times \tfrac{6}{30} + 7 \times \tfrac{7}{30} + 8 \times \tfrac{8}{30} = \tfrac{190}{30} = \tfrac{19}{3} = 6\tfrac{1}{3}$$

(b) $E(3X - 2) = 3E(X) - 2 = 19 - 2 = 17$

(c) $E(10 - X) = E(-X + 10) = -E(X) + 10 = -6\tfrac{1}{3} + 10 = 3\tfrac{2}{3}$

Example 5

The probability distribution of the discrete random variable R is shown in the table.

r	1	2	3	4
$P(R = r)$	0.2	0.4	0.3	0.1

(a) Write down the probability distribution for $12R^{-1}$.

(b) Find the value of   (i) $E(12R^{-1})$ (ii) $E(24R^{-1} + 5)$

Solution

(a) $12R^{-1} = \dfrac{12}{R}$. The four possible values of $12R^{-1}$ are $\frac{12}{1}, \frac{12}{2}, \frac{12}{3}, \frac{12}{4}$ or 12, 6, 4, 3.

So the probability distribution of $12R^{-1}$ is this:

Strictly speaking, this should be $P(12R^{-1} = 12r^{-1})$. ⟶

$12r^{-1}$	12	6	4	3
Probability	0.2	0.4	0.3	0.1

(b) (i) $E(12R^{-1}) = 12 \times 0.2 + 6 \times 0.4 + 4 \times 0.3 + 3 \times 0.1 = 6.3$

(ii) $24R^{-1} + 5$ is a linear function of $12R^{-1}$. It is $2(12R^{-1}) + 5$.

So $E(24R^{-1} + 5) = 2 \times 6.3 + 5 = 17.6$

Exercise C (answers p 117)

1 X is a discrete random variable for which $E(X) = 4.25$. Find the value of

(a) $E(3X)$ (b) $E(3X + 4)$ (c) $E(-2X)$ (d) $E(-2X + 7)$

2 The discrete random variable S has the probability distribution given in this table. Find

s	1	2	3	4
$P(S = s)$	0.2	0.4	0.3	0.1

(a) $E(S)$

(b) $E(3S + 2)$

(c) $E(8 - 2S)$

3 The probability distribution of a discrete random variable X is given by

$$P(X = x) = \begin{cases} k(x^2 - 3) & x = 2, 3, 4 \\ 0 & \text{otherwise} \end{cases}$$

Find **(a)** the value of k **(b)** $E(X)$ **(c)** $E(6 - X)$ **(d)** $E(5X - 1)$

4 The table shows the probability distribution of the discrete random variable X.

Find the value of

x	0	1	2	3	4
$P(X = x)$	0.1	0.25	0.3	0.2	0.15

(a) $E(X)$ **(b)** $E(X^2)$ **(c)** $E(X^3)$

5 The table shows the probability distribution of the discrete random variable X.

Find **(a)** $E(X^2)$ **(b)** $E(2X^2 - 1)$

x	1	2	3	4
$P(X = x)$	0.4	0.3	0.2	0.1

6 The probability distribution of the discrete random variable X is shown in this table.

x	0	1	2	3
$P(X = x)$	0.05	0.55	0.25	0.15

Find the value of $E\left(\dfrac{24}{X+1}\right)$.

7 The probability distribution of the discrete random variable T is given by

$$P(T = t) = \begin{cases} \dfrac{t^2}{55} & t = 1, 2, 3, 4, 5 \\ 0 & \text{otherwise} \end{cases}$$

Find the mean value of $60T^{-1}$.

D Variance and standard deviation (answers p 117)

D1 The probability distributions for the scores X and Y in two different games are given below.

Game A

x	0	1	2	3	4
$P(X = x)$	0.15	0.25	0.25	0.25	0.10

Game B

y	0	1	2	3	4
$P(Y = y)$	0.05	0.25	0.50	0.15	0.05

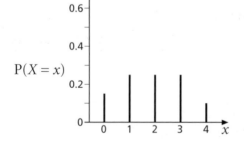

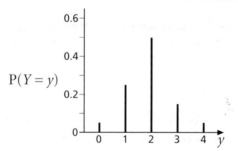

(a) Show that $E(X) = E(Y)$.

(b) The distributions are similar as far as the mean score is concerned. How do they differ?

The **variance** of the discrete random variable X is a measure of the spread of the distribution.

It is defined as $\sum(x_i - \mu)^2 p_i$, where μ stands for the mean value of X, or $E(X)$.

The variance of X is written as $\mathrm{Var}(X)$ and is often denoted by σ^2.

D2 For game A in question D1, $E(X) = \mu = 1.9$.

x	0	1	2	3	4
$P(X = x)$	0.15	0.25	0.25	0.25	0.10

So $\mathrm{Var}(X) = \sum(x_i - \mu)^2 p_i = (0 - 1.9)^2 \times 0.15 + (1 - 1.9)^2 \times 0.25 + \ldots$

Complete this calculation to find $\mathrm{Var}(X)$.

The definition $\sum(x_i - \mu)^2 p_i$ does not give the easiest way to calculate $\mathrm{Var}(X)$.
A simpler formula can be derived from the definition, as follows.

$$\begin{aligned}
\mathrm{Var}(X) &= \sum(x_i - \mu)^2 p_i \\
&= \sum(x_i^2 - 2\mu x_i + \mu^2) p_i && \textit{by expanding the brackets} \\
&= \sum x_i^2 p_i - 2\mu \sum x_i p_i + \mu^2 \sum p_i && \textit{by writing the single sum as three separate sums} \\
&= \sum x_i^2 p_i - 2\mu^2 + \mu^2 && \textit{because } \sum x_i p_i = \mu \text{ and } \sum p_i = 1 \\
&= \sum x_i^2 p_i - \mu^2
\end{aligned}$$

The expression $\sum x_i^2 p_i$ in this formula is the expression for $E(X^2)$.

So the formula may be written in a way that is easy to remember:

$\mathrm{Var}(X) = E(X^2) - [E(X)]^2$ 'variance = expectation of square – square of expectation'

The **standard deviation** σ is defined as $\sqrt{\mathrm{Var}(X)}$.

D3 For game B in question D1, $E(Y) = 1.9$.

y	0	1	2	3	4
$P(Y = y)$	0.05	0.25	0.50	0.15	0.05

(a) Find $E(Y^2)$.

(b) Use the formula $\mathrm{Var}(Y) = E(Y^2) - [E(Y)]^2$ to find the variance of Y.

(c) Which game has the greater variance? How could you tell this from the graphs?

Example 6

Find the variance and standard deviation of the random variable T whose probability distribution is given here.

t	0	1	2	3
$P(T = t)$	0.05	0.35	0.45	0.15

Solution

$\mathrm{Var}(T) = E(T^2) - [E(T)]^2$

$E(T) = \sum t_i p_i = (0 \times 0.05) + (1 \times 0.35) + (2 \times 0.45) + (3 \times 0.15) = 1.7$

$E(T^2) = \sum t_i^2 p_i = (0^2 \times 0.05) + (1^2 \times 0.35) + (2^2 \times 0.45) + (3^2 \times 0.15) = 3.5$

So $\mathrm{Var}(T) = E(T^2) - [E(T)]^2 = 3.5 - 1.7^2 = 0.61$

Standard deviation $= \sqrt{0.61} = 0.781$ to 3 d.p.

Exercise D (answers p 118)

1 The table shows the probability distribution of a
discrete random variable X. Find the value of

(a) $E(X)$ (b) $Var(X)$

x	0	1	2	3
$P(X = x)$	0.08	0.15	0.42	0.35

2 The table shows the probability distribution of
a discrete random variable S.
Find the value of   (a) $E(S)$ (b) $Var(S)$

x	1	2	3	4	5
$P(X = x)$	0.05	0.25	0.40	0.20	0.10

3 Find the mean and variance of the score obtained when this spinner
is spun once.

4 The probability distribution of a discrete random variable X is defined by

$$P(X = x) = \begin{cases} \frac{1}{20}x & x = 2, 3, 4, 5, 6 \\ 0 & \text{otherwise} \end{cases}$$

Find $E(X)$ and $Var(X)$.

5 The random variable U has the probability distribution
shown in the table. Given that $E(U) = 0.8$, find

(a) the values of a and b (b) $Var(U)$

u	0	1	2	3
$P(U = u)$	0.4	a	0.1	b

E Variance of a function of a discrete random variable (answers p 118)

E1 The probability distribution of a discrete random
variable X is shown in this table.

(a) Find $Var (X)$.

x	0	1	2	3
$P(X = x)$	0.1	0.3	0.4	0.2

Each possible value of X is doubled to give the
random variable Y, where $Y = 2X$.

y	0	2	4	6
$P(Y = y)$	0.1	0.3	0.4	0.2

(b) (i) Write down the value of $E(Y)$.

    (ii) Find $E(Y^2)$ and hence $Var(Y)$.

(c) Is the variance of Y double the variance of X?
If not, what is the relationship between $Var(Y)$ and $Var(X)$?

E2 The table shows the probability distribution of
a discrete random variable X.

(a) Find $Var(X)$.

x	0	1	2	3
$P(X = x)$	0.05	0.55	0.25	0.15

Let $Y = 3X + 2$.

(b) Before doing any calculation, write down what you think is the value of $Var(Y)$.

(c) Copy and complete this distribution
table for Y, and find $Var(Y)$.

y	2			
$P(Y = y)$	0.05	0.55	0.25	0.15

(d) How are $Var(Y)$ and $Var(X)$ related?

K The variance of a linear function $aX + b$ of the random variable X is related to the variance of X by the equation

$$\text{Var}(aX + b) = a^2\text{Var}(X)$$

The explanation is as follows.

(1) The variance, defined as $\sum(x_i - \mu)^2 p_i$, involves the squared deviations from the mean. If every value x_i is multiplied by a, the mean is also multiplied by a. So every deviation from the mean $(x_i - \mu)$ is also multiplied by a. When the deviations are squared, they are each multiplied by a^2. So the variance is multiplied by a^2.

(2) If b is added to every value x_i, it gets added to the mean as well. So the deviations from the mean $(x_i - \mu)$ do not change and so there is no effect on the variance.

(3) If we both multiply each value by a and then add b, the variance is multiplied by a^2 but, again, adding a constant to each value has no effect on the variance. So $\text{Var}(aX + b) = a^2\text{Var}(X)$.

E3 The table shows the probability distribution of a discrete random variable X.

x	1	2	3	4
$P(X = x)$	0.2	0.4	0.3	0.1

(a) Find $\text{Var}(X)$.

(b) Find   (i) $\text{Var}(4X)$ (ii) $\text{Var}(3X - 4)$

E4 With X defined as in the previous question, let $Y = \dfrac{12}{X}$. This is a non-linear function.

(a) Complete this table for the distribution of Y.

y	12	6		
$P(Y = y)$	0.2	0.4	0.3	0.1

(b) Find $E(Y)$ and $E(Y^2)$.

(c) Use the formula $\text{Var}(Y) = E(Y^2) - [E(Y)]^2$ to find $\text{Var}(Y)$.

(d) Use the result of E3(a) to show that $\text{Var}\left(\dfrac{12}{X}\right)$ is **not** equal to $\dfrac{12}{\text{Var}(X)}$.

K To find the variance of a non-linear function $g(X)$, use the formula

variance = expectation of square − square of expectation

with $g(X)$ instead of X.

For example, $\text{Var}\left(\dfrac{1}{X}\right) = E\left[\left(\dfrac{1}{X}\right)^2\right] - \left[E\left(\dfrac{1}{X}\right)\right]^2$

Example 7

The mean of the score of a single throw of a normal dice is 3.5 with variance $\frac{35}{12}$.
In a game, the score is doubled and 3 subtracted.
What are the mean and variance of the score in this game?

Solution

If X is the usual score, the new score is $2X - 3$.

$$E(2X - 3) = 2 \times 3.5 - 3 = 4 \qquad\qquad \text{Var}(2X - 3) = 2^2 \times \tfrac{35}{12} = \tfrac{35}{3}$$

Example 8

The probability distribution of the discrete random variable W is shown in the table.

w	0	1	2
$P(W = w)$	0.2	0.5	0.3

Find $\text{Var}(W^3)$.

Solution

You can work in terms of W^3 as given, but it is easier to use another letter, say Y, for W^3.

Let $Y = W^3$.

The probability distribution for Y is:

y	0	1	8
$P(Y = y)$	0.2	0.5	0.3

Use $\text{Var}(Y) = E(Y^2) - [E(Y)]^2$.

$E(Y) = (0 \times 0.2) + (1 \times 0.5) + (8 \times 0.3) = 2.9$

$E(Y^2) = (0^2 \times 0.2) + (1^2 \times 0.5) + (8^2 \times 0.3) = 19.7$

$\text{Var}(Y) = E(Y^2) - [E(Y)]^2 = 19.7 - 2.9^2 = 11.29$

Example 9

The discrete random variable S is such that $E(S) = 3$ and $\text{Var}(S) = 7.5$.

Find the value of   **(a)** $E(S^2)$ **(b)** $E[(S + 1)^2]$

Solution

(a) Use the formula $\text{Var}(S) = E(S^2) - (E(S))^2$.

$$\text{So } 7.5 = E(S^2) - 3^2, \text{ from which } E(S^2) = 16.5.$$

(b) $E[(S + 1)^2] = E(S^2 + 2S + 1)$

$= E(S^2) + E(2S + 1)$ *using 'expectation of sum = sum of expectations'*

$= E(S^2) + 2E(S) + 1 = 16.5 + 6 + 1 = 23.5$

Exercise E (answers p 118)

1 If X is the score on a single throw of a tetrahedral dice numbered 1–4, then $E(X) = 2.5$ and $\text{Var}(X) = 1.25$. Find

   (a) $E(3X)$ **(b)** $E(2X + 3)$ **(c)** $\text{Var}(2X)$ **(d)** $\text{Var}(3X + 2)$

2 X is a discrete random variable for which $E(X) = 1.5$ and $\text{Var}(X) = 0.18$. Find the value of

   (a) $E(4X)$ **(b)** $\text{Var}(4X)$ **(c)** $E\left(4 - \frac{1}{3}X\right)$ **(d)** $\text{Var}\left(4 - \frac{1}{3}X\right)$

3 The probability distribution of the discrete random variable X is given by

$$P(X = x) = \begin{cases} k(x + 2) & x = 0, 1, 2, 3, 4 \\ 0 & \text{otherwise} \end{cases}$$

   Find   **(a)** the value of k **(b)** $E(X)$ **(c)** $\text{Var}(X)$ **(d)** $\text{Var}(10 - 2X)$

4 A computer graphics program produces circles whose radius in cm is chosen at random from the numbers 1, 2, 3, 4, 5 with equal probabilities.

The discrete random variable S is the area in cm^2 of a circle produced by the program. Leaving π in your answer, find

(a) the mean value of S

(b) the variance of S

(c) the standard deviation of S

5 This table shows the probability distribution of the discrete random variable X. Find

x	1	2	3	4
$P(X = x)$	0.1	0.2	0.4	0.3

(a) $\text{Var}(X)$ (b) $\text{Var}(X^2)$ (c) $\text{Var}(24X^{-1})$

6 A discrete random variable X is such that $E(X) = 8$ and $\text{Var}(X) = 3$.
Another discrete random variable Y is defined by $Y = aX + b$.
Given that $E(Y) = 30$ and $\text{Var}(Y) = 27$, find the values of a and b.

7 T is a discrete random variable such that $E(T) = 5$, $E(T^2) = 35$ and $E(T^4) = 1250$.

(a) Show that Var $(T) = 10$.

(b) Show that Var $(T^2) = 25$.

8 The discrete random variable V is such that $E(V) = 2.5$ and $\text{Var}(V) = 4.25$.

(a) Show that $E(V^2) = 10.5$.

(b) Find the value of $E[V(V - 1)]$.

9 The discrete random variable W has the probability distribution shown in this table.

w	1	2	3	4	5
$P(W = w)$	0.1	0.2	0.3	0.25	0.15

(a) Find the value of

(i) $E(W)$ (ii) $E(W^2)$ (iii) $\text{Var}(W)$

A rectangle is drawn with sides of length W and $W + 10$ units.

(b) Write down an expression for the perimeter of the rectangle.

(c) Find the mean and variance of the perimeter of the rectangle.

(d) Show that the area of the rectangle is $W^2 + 10W$.

(e) Find the mean of the area of the rectangle.

10 The probability distribution for the discrete random variable R is tabulated below.

r	1	2	3	4	5
$P(R = r)$	0.1	0.2	0.4	0.2	0.1

(a) Given that $E(R) = 3$ and $\text{Var}(R) = 1.2$, find the mean and variance of $5(2R - 1)$.

(b) (i) Write down the probability distribution for $\dfrac{60}{R}$.

(ii) Show that $E\left(\dfrac{60}{R}\right) = 24.2$.

(iii) Given that $E\left(\dfrac{3600}{R^2}\right) = 759.4$, determine the variance of $\dfrac{60}{R}$.

AQA 2003

Key points

- A discrete random variable takes individual values (usually integers), each with a given probability.
  If X is any discrete random variable, then $\sum P(X = x) = 1$. (pp 6, 7)

- The expected value, expectation or mean of a discrete random variable X is denoted by $E(X)$ or μ. It is defined as $\sum x_i p_i$, where p_i is the probability of the value x_i. (p 9)

- If $g(X)$ is a function of the discrete random variable X, then $E[g(X)] = \sum g(x_i)p_i$. (p 14)

- $E[f(X) + g(X)] = E[f(X)] + E[g(X)]$ $E[kg(X)] = kE[g(X)]$ (p 14)

- The variance of X is defined by $\text{Var}(X) = \sum (x_i - \mu)^2 p_i$. It is often denoted by σ^2.
  $\text{Var}(X) = E(X^2) - [E(X)]^2$ (p 17)

- $E(aX + b) = aE(X) + b$ $\text{Var}(aX + b) = a^2\text{Var}(X)$ (pp 12, 19)

- To find $\text{Var}[g(X)]$, use the formula $\text{Var}(X) = E(X^2) - [E(X)]^2$ with $g(X)$ in place of X. (p 19)

Mixed questions (answers p 118)

1 The probability distribution of a discrete random variable X is shown in the table. Find

x	1	2	3	4	5
$P(X = x)$	0.1	0.2	0.3	0.3	0.1

(a) $E(X)$ (b) $\text{Var}(X)$ (c) $E(3X + 2)$ (d) $\text{Var}(2X - 6)$

2 The probability distribution of a discrete random variable X is given by

$$P(X = x) = \begin{cases} kx(8 - x) & x = 4, 5, 6, 7 \\ 0 & \text{otherwise} \end{cases}$$

where k is a positive constant.

(a) Find the value of k.   (b) Calculate $E(X)$.   (c) Calculate $\text{Var}(X)$.
(d) Find $E(3X - 2)$.   (e) Find $\text{Var}(3X - 2)$.

3 A dice is weighted so that the probability of getting a six is 0.55, and the other numbers are equally likely.

(a) Make a table for the probability distribution of the score on a single throw of this dice.

(b) Calculate the mean and variance of the score.

4 The discrete random variable X has the probability distribution shown in the table.
Given that $E(X) = 1.65$, find the values of

x	−1	0	1	2	3
$P(X = x)$	α	0.1	0.2	β	0.2

(a) α and β (b) $E(X^2)$ (c) $\text{Var}(X)$ (d) $E(2X - 1)$ (e) $\text{Var}(2X + 3)$

5 The discrete random variable X has the probability distribution shown in the table.

x	-2	-1	0	1	2
$P(X = x)$	α	0.3	β	0.1	0.2

Given that $E(X) = -0.1$, find the values of

(a) α and β (b) $E(X^2)$ (c) $Var(X)$ (d) $E(5 - X)$ (e) $Var(5 - X)$

6 A gambling machine is being designed. The payouts are to be £0, £2, £5 and £20.

The probability of paying out £2 has been fixed at 0.1 and the probability of paying out £5 has been fixed at 0.05.

The other probabilities have not yet been fixed: the probability of paying out £0 is a and the probability of paying out £20 is b.

X represents the payout per game. The probability distribution of X is shown here.

x	0	2	5	20
$P(X = x)$	a	0.1	0.05	b

(a) Find an expression for $E(X)$.

(b) The machine is fair to the player if the expected value of the payout is equal to the cost of a game. If the cost of a game is £1, what must the values of a and b be for the machine to be fair?

(c) It is decided to fix b at 0.01. The cost of a game is £1. What is the expected loss per game to the player?

7 A café owner installs two machines, A and B. On each machine a game costs £2. The payouts, £X on machine A and £Y on machine B, have the distributions below.

A

x	0	2	5	10	20
$P(X = x)$	0.70	0.10	0.10	0.09	0.01

B

y	0	2	5	10	20
$P(Y = y)$	0.82	0.05	0.05	0.02	0.06

(a) Find   (i) $E(X)$ (ii) $Var(X)$ (iii) $E(Y)$ (iv) $Var(Y)$

(b) Which machine is better from the player's point of view? Give the reason for your answer.

(c) How much does a player expect to lose, per game, on each machine?

(d) How can you tell by looking at the probability functions that the variance of Y is greater than the variance of X?

8 The discrete random variable T is such that $E(T) = 5$ and $Var(T) = 25$.

(a) A rectangle has sides of length $2T$ and $(T + 5)$. Determine the mean and variance of the **perimeter** of the rectangle.

(b) (i) Show that $E(T^2) = 50$.

(ii) Hence determine the mean of the **area** of the rectangle.   AQA 2002

9 The radius, R centimetres, of a circle in a computer-generated picture is a discrete random variable with $E(R) = 2$, $E(R^2) = 5$ and $Var(R) = 1$.

Determine, in terms of π,

(a) the mean and variance of the **circumference** of the circle

(b) the mean of the **area** of the circle   AQA 2002

Test yourself (answers p 119)

1 The probability distribution for the number of vehicles, V, involved in each minor accident on a particular stretch of road can be modelled as follows.

v	1	2	3	4	5
$P(V = v)$	0.15	0.45	0.20	0.15	0.05

(a) Show that $E(V) = 2.5$ and $Var(V) = 1.15$.

(b) The total cost, £C, of removing all the damaged vehicles following a minor accident is given by

$$C = 30V + 25$$

Determine the mean and variance of C.

(c) The total repair cost, £R, for all the vehicles involved in a minor accident is given by

$$R = 40V^2 + 15V + 50$$

Determine the value of $E(R)$.

AQA 2003

2 The discrete random variable R is such that $E(R) = 3$ and $Var(R) = 1$.

(a) Determine the mean and variance of $5(R - 1)$.

The probability distribution of R is

$$P(R = r) = \begin{cases} \dfrac{r}{10} & x = 1, 2, 3, 4 \\ 0 & \text{otherwise} \end{cases}$$

(b) Calculate the mean and variance of $12R^{-1}$.

AQA 2002

3 The probability distribution for the number, R, of unwrapped sweets in a tin is given in the following table.

r	1	2	3	4	5
$P(R = r)$	0.1	0.2	0.4	0.2	0.1

(a) Show that

(i) $E(R) = 3$

(ii) $Var(R) = 1.2$

(b) The number, P, of partially wrapped sweets in a tin is given by

$$P = 3R + 4$$

Find values for $E(P)$ and $Var(P)$.

(c) The total number of sweets in a tin is 200. Sweets are either correctly wrapped, partially wrapped or unwrapped.

(i) Express C, the number of correctly wrapped sweets in a tin, in terms of R.

(ii) Hence find the mean and variance of C.

AQA 2004

2 Poisson distribution

In this chapter you will learn
- how to calculate probabilities using the Poisson distribution
- how to find the mean and variance of a Poisson distribution
- about the additive property of the Poisson distribution

A The Poisson model (answers p 119)

An observer records the times at which cars go past on a country road.

Cars pass at random times. The times for the first two hours of observation are shown in the diagram below. The numbers below the diagram show how many cars passed during each 10-minute interval.

The number of cars passing in each 10-minute interval continued to be recorded. The complete record and a frequency table are shown here.

3 2 0 4 2 5 3 0 3 1 2 2 0 1 2 2 2 0 4 3 0 0 3 1 0

0 3 2 1 1 0 1 1 2 0 1 1 3 3 0 3 1 2 1 1 1 2 4 2 1

3 3 0 1 2 1 2 2 3 1 0 2 6 2 1 3 0 1 2 2 2 1 1 2 0

4 2 3 1 1 0 4 2 1 1 1 2 3 1 4 2 1 3 2 4 0 1 5 2 1

Number of cars in interval	Frequency
0	17
1	30
2	27
3	16
4	7
5	2
6	1
≥ 7	0
Total	100

The total number of cars is $0 \times 17 + 1 \times 30 + \ldots + 6 \times 1 = 176$.

So the mean number of cars per 10-minute interval is $\frac{176}{100} = 1.76$.

Let the discrete random variable X be the number of cars passing in a 10-minute interval.

The probability that $X = 0$ can be estimated from the data as $\frac{17}{100}$, or 0.17.
Similarly for the other possible values of X.

The probability distribution for X, based on the data, is shown here.

x	0	1	2	3	4	5	6	≥ 7
$P(X = x)$	0.17	0.30	0.27	0.16	0.07	0.02	0.01	0

Suppose that the mean number of cars in a 10-minute interval continues to be 1.76.

The French mathematical physicist Siméon Denis Poisson (1781–1840) suggested a mathematical model for events occurring randomly but with a constant mean rate:

$$P(X = x) = e^{-\lambda} \frac{\lambda^x}{x!}, \text{ where } \lambda \text{ is the mean value of } X \text{ (Note: 0! is taken to be 1.)}$$

A1 By letting $\lambda = 1.76$, find the probabilities for the cars data given by the Poisson model and compare them with the values in the table above.

K If events occur randomly but with a constant mean rate λ per time interval (per 10 minutes, per second, etc.), then the number X of events occurring in an interval can be modelled by the Poisson probability distribution given by

$$P(X = x) = e^{-\lambda}\frac{\lambda^x}{x!} \qquad x = 0, 1, 2, 3, \ldots$$

λ is called the Poisson parameter. When its value is known, the distribution is completely specified.

'X follows the Poisson distribution with parameter λ' is written as $X \sim Po(\lambda)$.

There is no limit on the possible values of X, but $P(X = x)$ gets smaller and smaller as x increases. It can be shown that the infinite sum $\sum P(X = x)$ is 1.

The shape of the Poisson distribution for different values of λ can be investigated by using a spreadsheet.

In Excel, e^x is denoted by EXP(x) and $x!$ by FACT(x).

Here are stick graphs for Poisson distributions with $\lambda = 0.75$, 2 and 5.

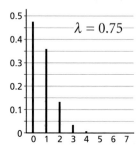 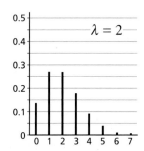 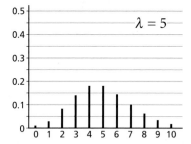

A2 Emissions from a radioactive source are detected by a Geiger counter. The emissions occur at random at a mean rate of 6 per second, so the number X of emissions in a 1-second period is such that $X \sim Po(6)$.

Calculate the probability that in a 1-second period the number of emissions is

(a) 5   (b) 6   (c) 7

The Poisson model can be used for other kinds of process involving random events.

For example when a machine produces a thread or yarn, knots may appear at random points along the length of the thread.

If the mean number of knots per metre is constant, then the number of knots appearing in a 1-metre interval has a Poisson distribution.

A3 Knots occur at random along the length of a thread with a mean rate of 3 knots per metre.

Find the probability that in a metre length of thread the number of knots is

(a) 0   (b) 1   (c) 2   (d) 3   (e) more than 3

The Poisson distribution as a limiting case of the binomial distribution

The Poisson distribution can be related to the binomial distribution.

We have seen how the Poisson model can be used for knots appearing in a thread.

Imagine instead that a chain is being produced, with n links in each metre. Instead of knots, faulty links (F) may occur.

Make the following assumptions:

- The probability that a link is faulty is p and is the same for every link.
- Whether a link is faulty or not is independent of any other link.

These are the conditions for the binomial distribution to apply.
The n links in a metre are the n 'trials' and the probability p that a link is faulty is the probability of 'success'.

Let X be the number of faulty links in a metre.
$P(X = x)$ is given by the binomial formula, so $P(X = x) = \binom{n}{x} p^x (1 - p)^{n-x}$.

The mean value of a binomial distribution is np. Let $np = \lambda$, so that $p = \dfrac{\lambda}{n}$.

The expression for $P(X = x)$ becomes $\binom{n}{x} \left(\dfrac{\lambda}{n}\right)^x \left(1 - \dfrac{\lambda}{n}\right)^{n-x}$.

It can be shown that, as n gets larger and larger (so that the chain becomes more and more like a thread), this expression gets closer and closer to the Poisson probability $e^{-\lambda} \dfrac{\lambda^x}{x!}$.

When n is large and p is small, the Poisson formula with $\lambda = np$ may be used as an approximation to the binomial formula.

Here, for example, are the first few binomial and Poisson probabilities with $n = 50$ and $p = 0.01$, so that $\lambda = np = 50 \times 0.01 = 0.5$.

	0	1	2	3
Binomial, B(50, 0.01)	0.6050	0.3056	0.0756	0.0122
Poisson, Po(0.5)	0.6065	0.3033	0.0758	0.0126

Example 1

Customers arrive at random at a checkout at the average rate of 2.4 per minute. What is the probability that in a one-minute period the number arriving is

(a) 0   (b) 1   (c) 2 or more

Solution

If the number arriving in one minute is X, then $X \sim \text{Po}(2.4)$.

(a) $P(X = 0) = e^{-2.4} \times \dfrac{2.4^0}{0!} = 0.091$ (to 3 d.p.)   (b) $P(X = 1) = e^{-2.4} \times \dfrac{2.4^1}{1!} = 0.218$ (to 3 d.p.)

(c) $P(X \geq 2) = 1 - P(X < 2) = 1 - (0.091 + 0.218) = 0.691$

Exercise A (answers p 119)

1 Given that $X \sim \text{Po}(1.5)$, calculate

    (a) $\text{P}(X = 0)$ **(b)** $\text{P}(X = 2)$ **(c)** $\text{P}(X \leq 3)$ **(d)** $\text{P}(X \geq 5)$

2 Incoming calls to a call centre arrive at random but have a constant average rate of 4.2 calls in a five-minute period. Find the probability that

    (a) there are no calls in a given five-minute period

    (b) there are exactly 3 calls in a five-minute period

    (c) there are more than 3 calls in a five-minute period

3 A botanist is investigating the number of buttercup plants on a field. A square frame, called a quadrat, is thrown at random on to the field and the number of buttercup plants inside is counted. The number of buttercups found per quadrat on the field can be modelled by a Poisson distribution with mean 3.4. Find the probability that in a particular quadrat there are

    (a) no buttercup plants   **(b)** more than 2 buttercup plants

4 A company makes windscreens for cars. Defects in the windscreens occur at random but at an average rate of 0.8 per windscreen. Use the Poisson distribution to find the probability that a windscreen inspected has

    (a) no defects   **(b)** 1 defect   **(c)** more than 1 defect

5 A newsagent buys in 5 copies of a particular magazine each week. The demand for this magazine each week can be modelled by a Poisson distribution with mean 2.5. Find the probability that, in a particular week,

    (a) nobody asks for a copy of this magazine

    (b) exactly three people ask for this magazine

    (c) more people ask for the magazine than the newsagent has copies

6 A proofreader is checking the pages of a book for misprints. Misprints occur at random at a mean rate of 1.2 per page.

    Find the probability that a particular page of the book

    (a) is free of misprints   **(b)** has 1 or 2 misprints   **(c)** has more than 2 misprints

7 **(a)** The random variable X is such that $X \sim \text{Po}(3)$. Find

        (i) $\text{P}(X = 3)$ **(ii)** $\text{P}(X = 2)$

    (b) The random variable Y is such that $Y \sim \text{Po}(5)$. Find

        (i) $\text{P}(Y = 5)$ **(ii)** $\text{P}(Y = 4)$

    (c) Show that if a random variable X is such that $X \sim \text{Po}(\lambda)$, where λ is an integer, then $\text{P}(X = \lambda) = \text{P}(X = \lambda - 1)$.

        (Two examples of this are apparent in the graphs on page 26.)

B The Poisson table (answers p 119)

In most applications of the Poisson distribution, λ is in the range $0 < \lambda \le 15$.

Tables are produced for the **cumulative** Poisson distribution for values of λ in this range.
The table for the exam is reproduced on pages 110–111 of this book.
It shows values of $P(X \le x)$, for each given value of λ.

The part of the table shown here includes the column for $\lambda = 1.8$.
It shows that if $X \sim \text{Po}(1.8)$, then $P(X \le 4) = 0.9636$.

To find $P(X = 4)$ we need to subtract $P(X \le 3)$ from $P(X \le 4)$:

$$P(X = 4) = P(X \le 4) - P(X \le 3)$$
$$= 0.9636 - 0.8913 = 0.0723$$

1.2	1.4	1.6	1.8	λ
				x
0.3012	0.2466	0.2019	0.1653	0
0.6626	0.5918	0.5249	0.4628	1
0.8795	0.8335	0.7834	0.7306	2
0.9662	0.9463	0.9212	0.8913	3
0.9923	0.9857	0.9763	0.9636	4
0.9985	0.9968	0.9940	0.9896	5
0.9997	0.9994	0.9987	0.9974	6
1.0000	0.9999	0.9997	0.9994	7
	1.0000	1.0000	0.9999	8
			1.0000	9

To find a probability of the form $P(X \ge x)$, for example $P(X \ge 4)$, use the fact that $P(X < 4) + P(X \ge 4) = 1$.

$$P(X < 4) = P(X \le 3) = 0.8913 \text{ so } P(X \ge 4) = 1 - 0.8913 = 0.1087$$

B1 The discrete random variable X has the Poisson distribution with parameter 1.4.
Use the table above to find

(a) $P(X \le 2)$ (b) $P(X = 2)$ (c) $P(X > 2)$ (d) $P(X \ge 2)$ (e) $P(1 \le X \le 3)$

B2 The discrete random variable Y has the Poisson distribution with parameter 1.6.
Use the table above to find

(a) $P(Y < 4)$ (b) $P(Y \ge 3)$ (c) $P(Y > 0)$ (d) $P(Y = 5)$ (e) $P(2 \le Y \le 5)$

Example 2

The discrete random variable X has the Poisson distribution with parameter 1.2.
Use the table to find

(a) $P(X = 2)$ (b) $P(X > 2)$ (c) $P(2 \le X \le 4)$

Solution

The table for $\lambda = 1.2$ is printed above.

(a) $P(X = 2) = P(X \le 2) - P(X \le 1) = 0.8795 - 0.6626 = 0.2169$

(b) $P(X > 2) = 1 - P(X \le 2) = 1 - 0.8795 = 0.1205$

(c) $P(2 \le X \le 4) = P(X \le 4) - P(X \le 1) = 0.9923 - 0.6626 = 0.3297$

Notice that, in each column, after a certain value of x the cumulative probability is recorded as 1.0000. This is because the values in the table are given to only four decimal places.

The Poisson formula gives a value of $P(X = x)$ for every possible value of x, but for large values of x these probabilities are very small. The cumulative probability gets closer and closer to 1 without ever reaching it, but this is not apparent when the values are rounded.

Exercise B (answers p 120)

Use the table on pages 110–111 to answer these questions.

1 The discrete random variable X has the Poisson distribution with $\lambda = 3.2$. Find

    (a) $P(X \le 5)$ **(b)** $P(X = 3)$ **(c)** $P(X \ge 3)$ **(d)** $P(X > 6)$ **(e)** $P(2 < X < 6)$

2 The number of call-outs in one hour to a breakdown repair service can be modelled by a Poisson distribution with mean 0.7. The service has three repair trucks that can be sent out. Find the probability that in any one-hour period

    (a) there are 2 or fewer call-outs

    (b) there are exactly 3 call-outs

    (c) there are more than 3 call-outs so the service cannot answer them all

3 A horticulturist is examining the leaves of a plant for viral spots. The number of spots on a leaf can be modelled by a Poisson distribution with mean 4.5. Find the probability that for a randomly chosen leaf

    (a) there are no spots   **(b)** there are exactly 3 spots

    (c) there are more than 5 spots

4 A factory has records showing that reported accidents happen on average 0.6 times per week. What is the probability that in a given week there are

    (a) no accidents   **(b)** more than 3 accidents

5 The number of applications for grants to an organisation can be modelled by a Poisson distribution with mean 3.2 per month. A maximum of 5 grants may be awarded in any one month. Find the probability that in a particular month

    (a) there are exactly 5 applications

    (b) there are more than 5 applications, so some have to be turned down

6 A local council is deciding whether to put a pedestrian crossing, controlled by traffic lights, at a point on a stretch of road. A survey showed that during the day cars pass by the point at random times but at a constant average rate of 6.5 per minute. Find the probability that in any given minute

    (a) 5 or fewer cars pass the point

    (b) more than 7 cars pass the point

7 A computer printer sometimes fails to print a sheet. The number of blank sheets per 100 can be modelled by a Poisson distribution with mean 2.4.

    Find the probability that out of 100 sheets fed into the printer

    (a) all are printed

    (b) all but one are printed

    (c) fewer than 97 are printed

C Mean, variance and standard deviation

If the discrete random variable X has the Poisson distribution with parameter λ, then the value of λ has already been identified as the mean value of X.

The mean value of X, or $E(X)$, is defined as $\sum x \times P(X = x)$.

When X is $Po(\lambda)$, this sum is $\sum x e^{-\lambda} \dfrac{\lambda^x}{x!}$ and it can be proved that this is equal to λ.

It can also be proved that $E(X^2) = \sum x^2 e^{-\lambda} \dfrac{\lambda^x}{x!} = \lambda^2 + \lambda$.

From the formula $Var(X) = E(X^2) - [E(X)]^2$ it follows that $Var(X) = \lambda^2 + \lambda - \lambda^2 = \lambda$.

> **K** If X has a Poisson distribution with parameter λ, then
> $$E(X) = \lambda$$
> $$Var(X) = \lambda \quad \text{(so the standard deviation is } \sqrt{\lambda})$$

Exercise C (answers p 120)

1 Bacteria occur at random in samples of water with a mean rate of 0.9 per ml.

  (a) Find the probability that a random sample of 1 ml of water contains no bacteria.

  (b) Find the probability that a random sample of 1 ml of water contains more than 5 bacteria.

  (c) Write down the variance of the number of bacteria in a random sample of 1 ml of water.

2 A machine produces a continuous length of steel wire. Kinks occur at random in the wire. The number of kinks occurring in 1 metre of wire has a Poisson distribution with parameter 6.5.

  (a) Write down the mean, variance and standard deviation of the number of kinks occurring in 1 metre of wire.

  (b) Find the probability that the number of kinks in 1 metre lies in the range from mean − standard deviation to mean + standard deviation.

3 A researcher noted the number of live births in the litters of a species of animal. For a very large sample of litters the following relative frequencies were found.

Number of live births	0	1	2	3	4	5	6	7	8
Relative frequency	0.14	0.23	0.26	0.15	0.10	0.06	0.03	0.02	0.01

  (a) From the data in the table, find the mean and variance of the number of live births in a litter.

  (b) Explain how you tell from your results in (a) that the data does not fit a Poisson distribution.

D Independent Poisson distributions

Suppose that cars going in one direction pass an observer at random times at a mean rate of 3 cars per minute. Independently, cars going in the other direction also pass at random times but at a mean rate of 2 cars per minute.

It seems intuitively obvious that cars, whichever direction they are going in, pass the observer at random times at a mean rate of 5 cars per minute.

If X is the number of cars passing in a one-minute interval in the first direction, then X is Po(3). If Y is the number passing in a one-minute interval in the opposite direction, then Y is Po(2).

If X and Y are independent (so that the value of each is unaffected by the other), it seems obvious that $X + Y$ will be Po(2 + 3), or Po(5).

It is possible to prove from the Poisson formula that this is true. The general result is as follows:

> If X and Y are independent random variables with Poisson distributions with parameters λ_1 and λ_2 respectively, then $X + Y$ has a Poisson distribution with parameter $\lambda_1 + \lambda_2$.

This property of the Poisson distribution allows us to combine intervals in an obvious way. For example, suppose that cars pass an observer at random times at a mean rate of 3 per minute. It is intuitively obvious that the mean number of cars in an interval of 5 minutes will be 15.

This can be confirmed as follows. Let X_1, X_2, X_3, X_4 and X_5 be the numbers passing in each of the five separate minutes making up a 5-minute interval. Each of these independent variables is Po(3), so the sum $X_1 + X_2 + X_3 + X_4 + X_5$ is Po(3 + 3 + 3 + 3 + 3), or Po(15).

Example 3

Cars on a production line are checked for mechanical faults and bodywork faults. Mechanical faults occur at random at a mean rate of 0.6 per car. Bodywork faults occur at random at a mean rate of 1.4 per car. The faults occur independently of each other. Find the probability that a randomly chosen car has

(a) no mechanical faults   (b) more than 3 faults of either type

Solution

(a) If M is the number of mechanical faults on a car then $M \sim$ Po(0.6).
$$P(M = 0) = e^{-0.6} = 0.5488$$

(b) If B is the number of bodywork faults on a car then $B \sim$ Po(1.4).
Let T be the total number of faults so that $T = M + B$.
Then $T \sim$ Po(0.6 +1.4), that is Po(2).

From the cumulative Poisson distribution table, $P(T \leq 3) = 0.8571$.
The probability that there are more than 3 faults is $1 - 0.8571 = 0.1429$.

Example 4

A typist makes mistakes randomly at an average rate of 1.2 per page.
Find the probability that in an article of 5 pages
(a) there are more than 10 mistakes in total
(b) there is at least one mistake on every page

Solution

(a) If X is the number of mistakes on a page, then $X \sim \text{Po}(1.2)$.
If Y is the number of mistakes on 5 pages then $Y \sim \text{Po}(5 \times 1.2)$, that is $\text{Po}(6)$.
From the cumulative Poisson distribution table $P(Y \leq 10) = 0.9574$.
So the probability of making more than 10 mistakes is $1 - 0.9574 = 0.0426$.

(b) The probability of at least one mistake on a single page is
$1 - P(X = 0) = 1 - 0.3012 = 0.6988$ (using $X \sim \text{Po}(1.2)$).
What happens on each page is independent of what happens on the others.
So the probability of at least one mistake on every page is $(0.6988)^5 = 0.1666$.

Checking the conditions for a Poisson model

The main condition for a Poisson model to be applicable is that events occur at
random but at a constant mean rate. For events to be random, each event must
be independent of any other event occurring. For example, arrivals at a cinema
for a family film would not be independent as people are likely to arrive in groups.

The assumption that there is a constant mean rate needs careful checking.
With cars on a stretch of road or arrivals at a supermarket, the mean rate of arrival
is likely to vary at different times of day. If the Poisson model is applied, it is
necessary to restrict it to a part of the day where the mean rate stays the same.

The Poisson model is a theoretical model and may not fit exactly the situation
it is applied to. For example, in the Poisson distribution there is no upper limit
on the possible values of the variable. In a situation such as cars passing an
observer, there is a physical limit to the number of cars that can pass, so the
Poisson model cannot be an exact fit.

Exercise D (answers p 120)

Use the table or the formula as appropriate.

1 Given that $X \sim \text{Po}(1.6)$ and $Y \sim \text{Po}(2.4)$, find
(a) $P(X \leq 3)$ (b) $P(Y = 5)$ (c) $P(X + Y \leq 6)$ (d) $P(X + Y > 6)$

2 The vehicles arriving at a petrol station are either private cars or commercial vans.
The number of cars arriving in a one-minute period can be modelled by
a Poisson distribution with mean 2.4.

(a) Find the probability that more than 6 cars arrive in a one-minute period.

The number of vans arriving in a one-minute period can be modelled by
a Poisson distribution with mean 0.8.

(b) Find the probability that more than 6 vehicles in total (cars or vans)
arrive in a one-minute period.

3 A keyboard operator enters customers' details on computerised forms.
He makes errors at random but on average he makes 1.5 errors per form.
Find the probability that on a particular form he makes

(a) no errors   (b) at least one error   (c) exactly one error

On a particular morning he completes three forms. Find the probability that

(d) there is a total of more than 5 errors

(e) there is at least one error on each form

4 A building society records information about each customer and about
the property (house or flat) that they live in. The customer information and
the property information are keyed in by two different operators.
Each operator makes errors at random. On average the first operator
makes 1.3 errors per customer and the second 1.8 errors per property.

Find the probability that there are more than 2 errors in total in the record for
a particular customer and their property.

5 The number of deaths in a year from the bite of a particular insect follows a
Poisson distribution with mean 4.0.
Find the probability that in a period of three years

(a) there are 10 or more deaths in total

(b) there are fewer than 3 deaths in each of the three years

6 An office has four computers that operate independently of each other.
For each computer, the number of breakdowns in a week is modelled by
a Poisson distribution with mean 0.8.

(a) Find the probability that in a particular week

    (i) none of the computers breaks down

    (ii) at least one computer breaks down

(b) Find the probability that in a period of four weeks

    (i) 2 or more computer breakdowns occur

    (ii) every computer breaks down at least once

7 A student suggests using the Poisson distribution to model the number of
telephone calls received per minute in an office with only one telephone.
Explain why the Poisson distribution is not appropriate in this case.

8 The number of vehicles arriving at a toll bridge during a 5-minute period
can be modelled by a Poisson distribution with mean 3.6.

(a) Calculate

    (i) the probability that at least 3 vehicles arrive in a 5-minute period

    (ii) the probability that at least 3 vehicles arrive in each of three
       successive 5-minute periods

(b) Show that the probability that no vehicles arrive in a 10-minute period
    is 0.0007, correct to four decimal places.   AQA 2002

Mixed questions (answers p 120)

1 Two roads converge at a junction. The number X of vehicles arriving per minute from the first road is such that $X \sim \text{Po}(2.8)$. The number Y arriving per minute from the second road is such that $Y \sim \text{Po}(3.2)$. X and Y are independent.

(a) Write down the distribution of $X + Y$, the total number arriving per minute at the junction.

(b) What is the variance of $X + Y$?

2 Outbreaks of a rare disease occur at random on average once in 50 years. Find the probability that

(a) there is no outbreak in the next 100 years

(b) there is at least one outbreak in the next 200 years

(c) there is no outbreak in the next 100 years but at least one in the 100 years after that

*3 Cars arrive at a river ferry at random times but at a constant mean rate of 4 cars in each hour. The ferry departs at one-hourly intervals and can carry up to 3 cars at a time. If the ferry is full then any cars not taken on board must wait in a queue until a space becomes available for them on a later ferry.

The 9 a.m. ferry has just departed. No car was left behind when it departed.

(a) Find the probability that

   (i) no cars will be left waiting after the 10 a.m. ferry departs

   (ii) no cars will be left waiting after the 10 a.m. ferry departs and no cars will be left waiting after the 11 a.m. ferry departs

   (iii) just one car will be left waiting after the 10 a.m. ferry departs but no cars will be left waiting after the 11 a.m. ferry departs

(b) Find the overall probability that no cars will be left waiting after the 11 a.m. ferry departs.

*4 Emissions from a radioactive source occur at random times at a mean rate of 0.2 per second. So the number of emissions in one second has a Poisson distribution with mean 0.2.

(a) What is the distribution of the number of emissions in

    (i) 2 seconds   (ii) 3 seconds   (iii) 4 seconds

The 'waiting time' is defined as the time between one emission and the next.

Suppose an emission has just occurred. The waiting time will be less than 1 second if at least one emission occurs in the first second after the emission that has just occurred.

(b) Find the probability that the waiting time is less than 1 second.

The waiting time will be less than 2 seconds if at least one emission occurs in the first 2 seconds after the emission that has just occurred.

(c) Find the probability that the waiting time is less than 2 seconds.

(d) Hence find the probability that the waiting time will be between 1 and 2 seconds.

(e) Find the probability that the waiting time will be between

    (i) 2 and 3 seconds   (ii) 3 and 4 seconds

Emissions from a radioactive source occur at random times at a mean rate of λ per second.

(f) Write down an expression for the mean number of emissions occurring in a period of t seconds.

(g) Show that the probability that the waiting time is between t seconds and $t + h$ seconds is $e^{-\lambda t}(1 - e^{-\lambda h})$.

Test yourself (answers p 121)

1 The number of misprints on a page of a newspaper follows a Poisson distribution with mean 2.2 per page. Use the Poisson formula to calculate the probability that a particular page contains

(a) no misprints

(b) exactly one misprint

(c) two or more misprints

2 The number of letters of complaint received by a department store follows a Poisson distribution with mean 6.5 per day. Find the probability that on a particular day

(a) 7 or fewer letters of complaint are received

(b) exactly 7 letters of complaint are received   AQA 2001

3 The number of people joining a checkout queue at a supermarket may be modelled by a Poisson distribution with a mean of 1.8 per minute. Find the probability that in a particular minute the number of people joining the queue is

   (a) one or fewer   (b) exactly 3   AQA 2003

4 The weekly number of ladders sold by a small DIY shop can be modelled by a Poisson distribution with mean 1.4. Find the probability that in a particular week the shop will sell

(a) 2 or fewer ladders

(b) exactly 4 ladders

(c) 2 or more ladders   AQA 2002

5 Karen is an engineer who is responsible for maintaining a textile machine during the night shift. She is called when the machine operator believes that the machine needs adjustment or repair.

(a) The number of times Karen is called during a night shift may be modelled by a Poisson distribution with mean 0.8. Find the probability that, on a particular shift, she is called

   (i) two or fewer times

   (ii) at least once

   (iii) exactly once

(b) Karen is now made responsible for 5 machines. These machines are operated independently. For each machine, the number of times she is called during a night shift may be modelled by a Poisson distribution with mean 0.8.

   (i) State the distribution of the total number of times she is called during a night shift.

   (ii) Find the probability that, during a night shift, she is called 5 or more times.

   (iii) Find the probability that, during a night shift she is called at least once to each of the 5 machines.   AQA 2003

6 Bronwen runs a post office in a large village. The number of registered letters posted at this office may be modelled by a Poisson distribution with mean 1.4 per day.

(a) Find the probability that at this post office

   (i) two or fewer registered letters are posted on a particular day

   (ii) a total of four or more registered letters are posted on two consecutive days

(b) The village also contains a post office run by Gopal. Here the number of registered letters posted may be modelled by a Poisson distribution with mean 2.4 per day.

Find the probability that, on a particular day, the number of registered letters posted at Gopal's post office is less than four.

(c) The numbers of registered letters posted at the two post offices are independent. Find the probability that, on a particular day, the total number of registered letters posted at the two post offices is more than six.

(d) Give one reason why the Poisson distribution might not provide a suitable model for the number of registered letters posted daily at a post office.   AQA 2002

3 Continuous random variables

In this chapter you will learn
- what is meant by the probability density function and the distribution function of a continuous random variable
- how to use these functions to find probabilities, median, quartiles and percentiles
- how to find the mean, variance and standard deviation of a continuous random variable and of a function of a continuous random variable

A Probability density function (answers p 121)

Imagine that a bus is due to arrive at some time in an interval of 5 minutes. Its arrival time is equally likely to be anywhere in the interval.

The situation can be represented by this diagram. The area of the shaded rectangle is 1 and represents the total probability that the arrival time will lie somewhere in the interval of 5 minutes.

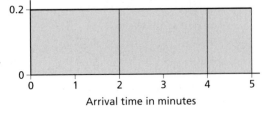

The area between 2 and 4 minutes represents the probability that the arrival time is between 2 and 4 minutes.
This probability is 0.4.

Now suppose that the bus is more likely to arrive near the middle of the interval than near either end.

This can be shown by changing the shape of the shaded area without changing the area itself, which is still 1.

As before, the area between 2 and 4 minutes shows the probability that the arrival time is between 2 and 4 minutes.

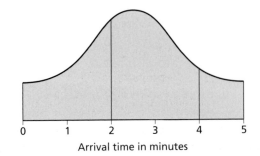

To find this probability we need to know more about the shape of the curve.

The arrival time is an example of a **continuous random variable**.

The curve shows its **probability density function**.

The arrival time in this example is confined to an interval of length 5 minutes. However, a continuous random variable may be able to take any value, positive or negative. In this case the probability density function will be defined for all values. The area under the curve is still 1. (The normal distribution is an example.)

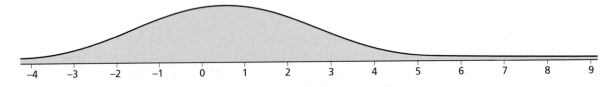

The following two statements are true for every probability density function f(x):

- f(x) ≥ 0 for all x (because probability cannot be negative).
- The total area under the graph of f(x) is 1 (because the total probability of all possible values is 1).

The second of these statements can be written as $\int_{-\infty}^{\infty} f(x)\,dx = 1$.

The symbol ∞ stands for 'infinity'. The x-axis is thought of as extending from −∞ to ∞.

In many cases, f(x) is zero outside a finite interval. For example, here is the graph of a probability density function which is zero outside the interval −1 ≤ x ≤ 1.

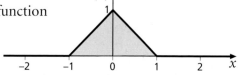

In this case, $\int_{-1}^{1} f(x)\,dx = 1$.

A1 The function f(x) is defined as follows:

$$f(x) = \begin{cases} 2(1-x) & 0 \le x \le 1 \\ 0 & \text{otherwise} \end{cases}$$

The graph of f(x) is shown in the diagram.

Show that the area under the graph is 1.

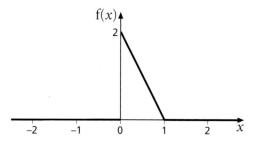

A2 The function f(x) is defined as follows:

$$f(x) = \begin{cases} k(4 - x^2) & 0 \le x \le 2 \\ 0 & \text{otherwise} \end{cases}$$

(a) Sketch the graph of f(x).

(b) Show by integration that the area under the graph is $\frac{16k}{3}$.

(c) Given that f(x) is a probability density function, state the value of k.

If the continuous random variable X has the probability density function f(x), the probability that X lies in the interval $a < x < b$ is the area under the graph of f(x) between a and b.

This can be written $P(a < X < b) = \int_a^b f(x)\,dx$.

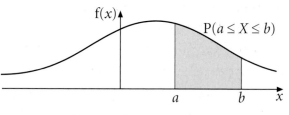

It doesn't matter whether the interval is written with < or with ≤, because P(X = a) = 0 for any individual value a. This is because the area under the graph from a to a is 0.

(Think of the bus example. What is the probability that the bus arrives at exactly, say, 3.275 087 minutes?)

A3 The continuous random variable X has the probability density function f(x) defined as in question A1. Find $P(0 \le X \le 0.5)$.

A4 The continuous random variable X has the probability density function f(x) defined as in question A2. Show that $P(0 \le X \le 1) = \frac{11}{16}$.

A5 The continuous random variable X has the probability density function given by

$$f(x) = \begin{cases} 6x(1-x) & 0 \le x \le 1 \\ 0 & \text{otherwise} \end{cases}$$

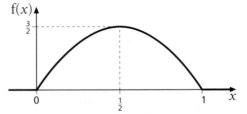

(a) Verify that the area under the graph of f(x) is 1.

(b) Find $P(0 \le X \le 0.4)$.

(c) Find $P(0.4 \le X \le 0.6)$.

A6 The continuous random variable X has the probability density function given by

$$f(x) = \begin{cases} kx(2-x) & 0 \le x \le 2 \\ 0 & \text{otherwise} \end{cases}$$

(a) Sketch the graph of f(x).

(b) Show by integration that the area under the graph is $\dfrac{4k}{3}$.

(c) Hence find the value of k.

(d) Explain why $P(X \le 1.5)$ is equal to $P(0 \le X \le 1.5)$ and find its value.

(e) Write down the value of $P(X > 1.5)$.

A probability density function may not be given by a single formula.
For example, this probability density function is made up of two parts:

$$f(x) = \begin{cases} \frac{3}{4}x^2 & 0 \le x \le 1 \\ \frac{3}{8}(3-x) & 1 \le x \le 3 \\ 0 & \text{otherwise} \end{cases}$$

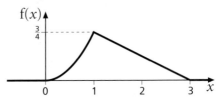

A7 (a) The area under the graph of f(x) shown above is made up of two parts:

$$\int_0^1 \tfrac{3}{4}x^2 \, dx + \int_1^3 \tfrac{3}{8}(3-x) \, dx$$

Verify that the area under the graph of f(x) is 1.

(b) Let X be a continuous random variable with the probability density function f(x) given above. Then $P(0.5 \le X \le 2)$ is made up of two parts:

$$\int_{0.5}^1 \tfrac{3}{4}x^2 \, dx + \int_1^2 \tfrac{3}{8}(3-x) \, dx$$

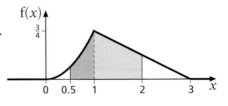

Find $P(0.5 \le X \le 2)$.

K If f(x) is the probability density function of the continuous random variable X, then

$$\int_{-\infty}^{\infty} f(x) \, dx = 1$$

$$P(a \le X \le b) = \int_a^b f(x) \, dx$$

$P(X = a) = 0$ (so that, for example, $P(a < X < b) = P(a \le X \le b)$)

Example 1

The continuous random variable X has the probability density function given by

$$f(x) = \begin{cases} kx^2 & 0 \le x \le 2 \\ 0 & \text{otherwise} \end{cases}$$

(a) Sketch the graph of f(x).

(b) Find the value of k.

(c) Find $P(X \le 1)$.

Solution

(a) The sketch is shown on the right.

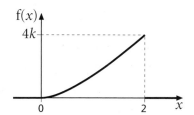

(b) Area under graph of probability density function

$$= \int_0^2 kx^2 \, dx = k\left[\tfrac{1}{3}x^3\right]_0^2 = \tfrac{8}{3}k$$

Area $= 1$, so $\tfrac{8}{3}k = 1$, so $k = \tfrac{3}{8}$

(c) $P(X \le 1) = P(0 \le X \le 1) = \int_0^1 \tfrac{3}{8}x^2 \, dx = \tfrac{3}{8}\left[\tfrac{1}{3}x^3\right]_0^1 = \tfrac{3}{8} \times \tfrac{1}{3} = \tfrac{1}{8}$

Example 2

The continuous random variable T has the probability density function given by

$$f(t) = \begin{cases} kt(4-t) & 0 \le t \le 2 \\ k(6-t) & 2 \le t \le 6 \\ 0 & \text{otherwise} \end{cases}$$

(a) Find the value of k.

(b) Find $P(T > 1)$.

Solution

(a) Area under graph of $f(t) = \int_0^2 kt(4-t)\,dt + \int_2^6 k(6-t)\,dt$

$$= k\int_0^2 (4t - t^2)\,dt + k\int_2^6 (6-t)\,dt$$

$$= k\left[2t^2 - \tfrac{1}{3}t^3\right]_0^2 + k\left[6t - \tfrac{1}{2}t^2\right]_2^6$$

$$= k(8 - \tfrac{8}{3}) + k[(36-18)-(12-2)] = \tfrac{40}{3}k$$

$\tfrac{40}{3}k = 1$, so $k = \tfrac{3}{40}$.

(b) *It is easiest to find* $P(T < 1)$ *and subtract it from 1.*

$$P(T < 1) = \int_0^1 \tfrac{3}{40}t(4-t)\,dt$$

$$= \tfrac{3}{40}\left[2t^2 - \tfrac{1}{3}t^3\right]_0^1 = \tfrac{3}{40} \times \tfrac{5}{3} = \tfrac{1}{8}$$

So $P(T > 1) = 1 - \tfrac{1}{8} = \tfrac{7}{8}$

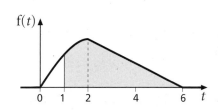

Exercise A (answers p 122)

1 The continuous random variable X has the probability density function $f(x)$ given by

$$f(x) = \begin{cases} \frac{1}{18}(9 - x^2) & 0 \le x \le 3 \\ 0 & \text{otherwise} \end{cases}$$

(a) Sketch the graph of $f(x)$.

(b) Verify that the area under the graph of $f(x)$ is 1.

(c) Find   (i) $P(0 \le X \le 1)$ (ii) $P(1 < X < 2)$ (iii) $P(X > 2)$

2 The continuous random variable X has the probability density function $f(x)$ given by

$$f(x) = \begin{cases} k(2 - x) & 0 \le x \le 2 \\ 0 & \text{otherwise} \end{cases}$$

(a) Sketch the graph of $f(x)$.   (b) Find the value of k.

(c) Find $P(1 \le X \le 2)$.

3 The continuous random variable X has the probability density function given by

$$f(x) = \begin{cases} kx(4 - x) & 0 \le x \le 4 \\ 0 & \text{otherwise} \end{cases}$$

(a) Sketch the graph of $f(x)$.   (b) Find the value of k.

(c) Find $P(X < 3)$.

4 The continuous random variable S has the probability density function given by

$$f(s) = \begin{cases} ks & 0 \le s < 4 \\ \frac{2}{3}k(10 - s) & 4 \le s < 10 \\ 0 & \text{otherwise} \end{cases}$$

(a) Sketch the graph of $f(s)$.

(b) Show that the area under the graph of $f(s)$ is $20k$.

(c) Hence find the value of k.

(d) Find $P(3 \le S \le 5)$.

5 The continuous random variable X has the probability density function given by

$$f(x) = \begin{cases} kx(x - 2)^2 & 0 \le x \le 2 \\ 0 & \text{otherwise} \end{cases}$$

(a) Find the value of k.   (b) Find $P(X > 1)$.

6 The continuous random variable T has the probability density function given by

$$f(t) = \begin{cases} kt^2 & 0 \le t < 3 \\ k(6 - t)^2 & 3 \le t < 6 \\ 0 & \text{otherwise} \end{cases}$$

(a) Sketch the graph of $f(t)$.   (b) Show that $k = \frac{1}{18}$.

(c) Find $P(2 \le T \le 5)$.

B Distribution function (answers p 122)

The diagram shows the probability density function $f(x)$ of a continuous random variable X given by

$$f(x) = \begin{cases} \frac{3}{4}x(2-x) & 0 \le x \le 2 \\ 0 & \text{otherwise} \end{cases}$$

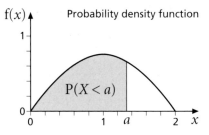

Probability density function

The shaded area represents the probability that the value of the random variable is less than a, that is $P(X < a)$.

B1 $P(X < a) = \int_0^a f(x)\,dx = \int_0^a \frac{3}{4}x(2-x)\,dx$.

Do the integration and show that the result can be written as $\frac{1}{4}a^2(3-a)$.

The expression $\frac{1}{4}a^2(3-a)$, which gives the probability that $X < a$, is a function of a. This function is called the **distribution function** of X.

It is usually written using x rather than a and is denoted by $F(x)$.

$$F(x) = P(X < x) = \frac{1}{4}x^2(3-x) \quad (0 \le x \le 2)$$

The graph of $F(x)$ is shown on the right.

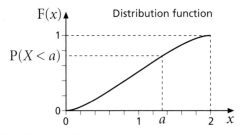

Distribution function

(The reason for using a rather than x when finding the distribution function is that it is incorrect to use the same letter, x, both for the function being integrated and for one of the limits of integration: $\int_0^x f(x)\,dx$ is not allowed. So do the integration with a as upper limit and then rewrite the result using x. Alternatively, change $f(x)\,dx$ to $f(t)\,dt$, then x can be the upper limit: $\int_0^x f(t)\,dt$.)

K The distribution function $F(x)$ of a random variable X is defined by $F(x) = P(X < x)$.

B2 The continuous random variable X has the probability density function given by

$$f(x) = \begin{cases} 0.08x & 0 \le x \le 5 \\ 0 & \text{otherwise} \end{cases}$$

(a) Sketch the graph of $f(x)$.

(b) Find $\int_0^a f(x)\,dx$.

(c) Hence state the distribution function of X in the form $F(x) = \ldots$

(d) Use the distribution function to find $P(X < 2.5)$.

B3 The continuous random variable S has the probability density function given by

$$f(s) = \begin{cases} 0.003s^2 & 0 \le s \le 10 \\ 0 & \text{otherwise} \end{cases}$$

(a) Find the distribution function $F(s)$ for S.   (b) Find $P(S < 8)$.

Just as F is the integral of f, so f is the derivative of F:

$$f(x) = F'(x) \quad \text{or} \quad f(x) = \frac{d}{dx} F(x)$$

B4 The distribution function of a continuous random variable X is given by
$F(x) = \frac{1}{2}x - \frac{1}{16}x^2 \ (0 \le x \le 4)$. Find the probability density function f(x).

Example 3

The probability density function of the continuous random variable T is given by

$$f(t) = \begin{cases} 0.012(25 - t^2) & 0 \le t \le 5 \\ 0 & \text{otherwise} \end{cases}$$

(a) Sketch the graph of f.

(b) Determine the distribution function F(t).

(c) Find $P(T \ge 2)$.

Solution

(a) The graph is quadratic.
  $f(0) = 0.012 \times 25 = 0.3$
  $f(5) = 0.012 \times (25 - 5^2) = 0$

(b) Let a be a value of t between 0 and 5.

$$F(a) = P(T < a) = \int_0^a 0.012(25 - t^2)\,dt = 0.012\left[25t - \tfrac{1}{3}t^3\right]_0^a$$

$$= 0.012\left(25a - \tfrac{1}{3}a^3\right) = 0.3a - 0.004a^3$$

So $F(t) = 0.3t - 0.004t^3 \ (0 \le t \le 5)$

(c) $P(T \ge 2) = 1 - P(T < 2) = 1 - F(2) = 1 - (0.3 \times 2 - 0.004 \times 2^3) = 0.432$

Exercise B (answers p 122)

1 For each probability density function below,

    (i) determine the distribution function F(x)   (ii) find $P(X < 1)$

(a) $f(x) = \begin{cases} 0.02x & 0 \le x \le 10 \\ 0 & \text{otherwise} \end{cases}$

(b) $f(x) = \begin{cases} 0.08(5 - x) & 0 \le x \le 5 \\ 0 & \text{otherwise} \end{cases}$

(c) $f(x) = \begin{cases} 0.024x^2 & 0 \le x \le 5 \\ 0 & \text{otherwise} \end{cases}$

(d) $f(x) = \begin{cases} \frac{3}{16}x(4 - x) & 0 \le x \le 2 \\ 0 & \text{otherwise} \end{cases}$

2 For each distribution function below,

    (i) find $P(X \ge 1)$ (ii) determine the probability density function

(a) $F(x) = \frac{1}{4}x^2 \ (0 \le x \le 2)$ (b) $F(x) = \frac{1}{4}x^2(3 - x) \ (0 \le x \le 2)$

C Median, quartiles and percentiles (answers p 122)

The arrival time of a bus is modelled by the continuous random variable X whose probability density function $f(x)$ is given by

$$f(x) = \begin{cases} \frac{1}{9}x^2 & 0 \leq x \leq 3 \\ 0 & \text{otherwise} \end{cases}$$

The graph of $f(x)$ is shown on the right.

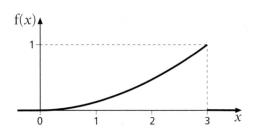

C1 Verify that the area under the graph is 1.

The **median** arrival time is the value that divides the area under the graph in half. So if m is the median,

$$P(X < m) = \tfrac{1}{2}$$

or $\displaystyle\int_0^m f(x)\,dx = \tfrac{1}{2}$

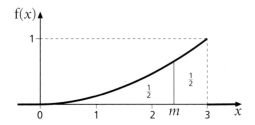

C2 For the random variable X, $\displaystyle\int_0^m f(x)\,dx = \int_0^m \tfrac{1}{9}x^2\,dx$.

(a) Find $\displaystyle\int_0^m \tfrac{1}{9}x^2\,dx$ in terms of m.

(b) Hence find the median, the value of m for which $P(X < m) = \tfrac{1}{2}$.

The **quartiles** of the distribution of X are the values that divide the area under the graph into quarters.

If l is the lower quartile, $P(X < l) = \tfrac{1}{4}$.

If u is the upper quartile, $P(X < u) = \tfrac{3}{4}$.

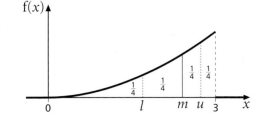

C3 (a) Solve the equation $\displaystyle\int_0^l \tfrac{1}{9}x^2\,dx = \tfrac{1}{4}$ to find the lower quartile.

(b) Find the upper quartile.

The 20th **percentile** of the distribution is the value that has 20% of the area below it. Similarly for other percentiles.

So if p_{20} is the 20th percentile, $P(X < p_{20}) = 0.20$.

C4 (a) Find the 20th percentile of the distribution of X.

(b) Find the 80th percentile.

K If X is a continuous random variable, then

$P(X < \text{median}) = \tfrac{1}{2}$ $P(X < \text{lower quartile}) = \tfrac{1}{4}$ $P(X < \text{upper quartile}) = \tfrac{3}{4}$

$P(X < \text{20th percentile}) = 0.20$, etc.

C5 This probability density function is made up of two parts:

$$f(x) = \begin{cases} \frac{1}{5}x & 0 \le x < 2 \\ \frac{2}{15}(5-x) & 2 \le x < 5 \\ 0 & \text{otherwise} \end{cases}$$

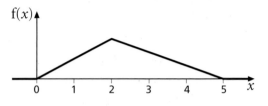

(a) Verify that the total area under the graph of f(x) is 1.

(b) Is the median m to the left or to the right of the value 2?

(c) By finding an expression for the area between $x = m$ and $x = 5$, or otherwise, find the value of m.

(d) Find the values of the lower and upper quartiles.

The median, quartiles and percentiles can all be related to the distribution function F.

For example, the median m is the value for which $F(m) = \frac{1}{2}$.

This is shown in the diagrams.

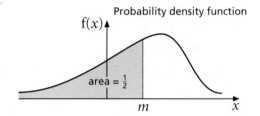

Probability density function

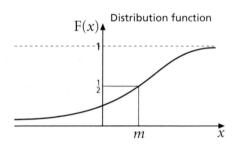

Distribution function

Similarly, if l and u are the lower and upper quartiles, then $F(l) = \frac{1}{4}$ and $F(u) = \frac{3}{4}$.

C6 The distribution function of a continuous random variable S is given by

$$F(s) = 0.04s(10 - s) \quad (0 \le s \le 5)$$

(a) Show that the upper quartile u satisfies the quadratic equation

$$4u^2 - 40u + 75 = 0$$

(b) By factorising this equation, or otherwise, find the value of u.

(c) If p is the 64th percentile then $F(p) = 0.64$.
Find the value of p.

Example 4

The continuous random variable X has the probability density function given by

$$f(x) = \begin{cases} \frac{1}{108}x^2 & 0 \le x < 6 \\ \frac{1}{6}(8-x) & 6 \le x < 8 \\ 0 & \text{otherwise} \end{cases}$$

(a) Sketch the graph of $f(x)$.

(b) Find $P(3 \le X < 7)$.

(c) Find the median value of X.

Solution

(a) *It is a good idea to sketch the graph, even if you are not asked to.*

The first part of the graph is quadratic and goes from $(0, 0)$ to $\left(6, \frac{1}{3}\right)$.

The second part is linear and goes from $\left(6, \frac{1}{3}\right)$ to $(8, 0)$.

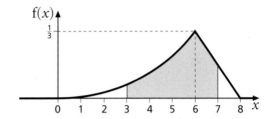

(b) $P(3 \le X < 7)$ is shown by the shaded area.

This can be calculated in two parts as $\int_3^6 \frac{1}{108}x^2\,dx + \int_6^7 \frac{1}{6}(8-x)\,dx$.

However, it is slightly easier to find the unshaded area and subtract this from 1, because one of the limits of the first integral is then 0.

Unshaded area $= \int_0^3 \frac{1}{108}x^2\,dx + \int_7^8 \frac{1}{6}(8-x)\,dx$

$\qquad = \frac{1}{108}\left[\frac{1}{3}x^3\right]_0^3 + \frac{1}{6}\left[8x - \frac{1}{2}x^2\right]_7^8$

$\qquad = \frac{1}{12} + \frac{1}{6}\left[(64-32)-\left(56-\frac{49}{2}\right)\right] = \frac{1}{6}$

Shaded area $= 1 - \frac{1}{6} = \frac{5}{6}$

(c) The area from 0 to 6 is $\int_0^6 \frac{1}{108}x^2\,dx = \frac{1}{108}\left[\frac{1}{3}x^3\right]_0^6 = \frac{2}{3}$, so the median m lies between 0 and 6.

$\int_0^m \frac{1}{108}x^2\,dx = \frac{1}{2} \;\Rightarrow\; \frac{1}{108}\left[\frac{1}{3}x^3\right]_0^m = \frac{1}{2} \;\Rightarrow\; m^3 = 162 \;\Rightarrow\; m = \sqrt[3]{162} = 5.45 \text{ (to 3 s.f.)}$

Exercise C (answers p 123)

1 The continuous random variable X has the probability density function given by

$$f(x) = \begin{cases} 0.08x & 0 \le x \le 5 \\ 0 & \text{otherwise} \end{cases}$$

(a) Sketch the graph of $f(x)$.   (b) Find the median of X.

(c) Find the lower quartile of X.   (d) Find the 80th percentile of X.

2 The continuous random variable T has the probability density function given by

$$f(t) = \begin{cases} kt^3 & 0 \le t \le 3 \\ 0 & \text{otherwise} \end{cases}$$

(a) Sketch the graph of f(t).   (b) Find the value of k.

(c) Find the median of T.   (d) Find the lower quartile of T.

3 The diagram shows the graph of the probability density function f(x) of the continuous random variable X.

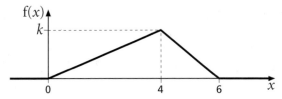

(a) Show that $k = \frac{1}{3}$.

(b) Find the equation for f(x) when $0 \le x \le 4$.

(c) Show that $f(x) = 1 - \frac{1}{6}x$ when $4 \le x \le 6$.

(d) Find

     (i) the median of X (ii) the lower quartile of X (iii) the upper quartile of X

4 The continuous random variable U has the probability density function given by

$$f(u) = \begin{cases} \frac{1}{24}(8-u) & 0 \le u \le 4 \\ 0 & \text{otherwise} \end{cases}$$

(a) Given that m is the median value of U, show that m satisfies the equation

$$m^2 - 16m + 24 = 0$$

(b) Find the value of m correct to one decimal place.

5 A student is making a study of vehicles passing a point on a road.
She models the time interval in minutes between one car and the next as a continuous random variable T with the probability density function given by

$$f(t) = \begin{cases} kt(16 - t^2) & 0 \le t \le 4 \\ 0 & \text{otherwise} \end{cases}$$

(a) Sketch the graph of f(t).

(b) Find the value of k.

(c) (i) Show that the median m satisfies the equation $m^4 - 32m^2 + 128 = 0$.

     (ii) By letting $x = m^2$, or otherwise, solve this equation, giving the value of m correct to one decimal place.

D Mean or expected value (answers p 124)

It is useful at this stage to compare discrete and continuous random variables.

The probability distribution of a discrete random variable X can be represented by a 'stick graph'. The probability p_i of each possible value x_i is shown by the height of the stick.

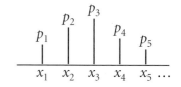

$$\sum p_i = 1$$

The probability distribution of a continuous random variable X is shown by a probability density function $f(x)$. The probability that the value of the variable lies in the interval from a to b is shown by the area under that part of the graph.

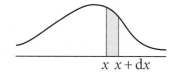

$$\int_{-\infty}^{\infty} f(x)\,dx = 1$$

You can think of the expression $f(x)\,dx$ as the probability that X lies in the small interval from x to $x + dx$.

The expression $f(x)\,dx$ behaves like p_i in the discrete case, except that integration $\int$ replaces summation $\sum$.

The mean or expected value of a discrete random variable X is defined by

$$E(X) = \sum x_i p_i$$

The corresponding definition for a continuous random variable X is

$$E(X) = \int_{-\infty}^{\infty} x f(x)\,dx$$

As you can see, p_i has been replaced by $f(x)\,dx$ and $\sum$ by $\int$.

Although the limits of integration are shown as $-\infty$ and ∞, in many cases the probability density function is zero outside a finite interval, so the limits will be the end-points of this interval.

For example, suppose the probability density function of X is given by

$$f(x) = \begin{cases} \frac{1}{2}x & 0 \le x \le 2 \\ 0 & \text{otherwise} \end{cases}$$

Then $E(X) = \int_{0}^{2} x\left(\frac{1}{2}x\right)dx = \frac{1}{2}\int_{0}^{2} x^2\,dx$

D1 (a) Complete this integration to find the value of $E(X)$.

    (b) How can you tell from the shape of the graph of $f(x)$ that the mean of X must be closer to 2 than to 0?

D2 A continuous random variable X has the probability density function given by

$$f(x) = \begin{cases} \frac{1}{9}x^2 & 0 \le x \le 3 \\ 0 & \text{otherwise} \end{cases}$$

Find $E(X)$.

The mean or expected value of the continuous random variable X is given by

$$E(X) = \int x\, f(x)\, dx$$

The integral is a definite integral, but the limits are not shown because they depend on the definition of $f(x)$.

If the probability density function is not given by a single formula, the integration has to be carried out separately for each part.

For example, suppose X has this probability density function:

$$f(x) = \begin{cases} \frac{1}{5}x & 0 \le x < 2 \\ \frac{2}{15}(5-x) & 2 \le x < 5 \\ 0 & \text{otherwise} \end{cases}$$

Then $E(X) = \int_0^2 x\left(\frac{1}{5}x\right) dx + \int_2^5 x\left(\frac{2}{15}(5-x)\right) dx$

D3 Complete this calculation of the value of $E(X)$.

Example 5

The time taken to complete a task is modelled by the continuous random variable T whose probability density function is given by

$$f(t) = \begin{cases} \frac{1}{36}t(6-t) & 0 \le t < 3 \\ \frac{1}{4} & 3 \le t < 5 \\ 0 & \text{otherwise} \end{cases}$$

Find the value of $E(T)$.

Solution

$$E(T) = \int t\, f(t)\, dt = \int_0^3 t\left(\frac{1}{36}t(6-t)\right) dt + \int_3^5 t\left(\frac{1}{4}\right) dt$$

$$= \frac{1}{36}\int_0^3 \left(6t^2 - t^3\right) dt + \frac{1}{4}\int_3^5 t\, dt$$

$$= \frac{1}{36}\left[2t^3 - \frac{1}{4}t^4\right]_0^3 + \frac{1}{4}\left[\frac{1}{2}t^2\right]_3^5$$

$$= \frac{1}{36}\left(54 - \frac{81}{4}\right) + \frac{1}{4}\left(\frac{25}{2} - \frac{9}{2}\right) = \frac{3}{2} - \frac{9}{16} + 2 = 2\frac{15}{16}$$

Exercise D (answers p 124)

1 The continuous random variable X has the probability density function given by

$$f(x) = \begin{cases} \frac{1}{24}(8-x) & 0 \le x \le 4 \\ 0 & \text{otherwise} \end{cases}$$

Find the value of $E(X)$.

2 The continuous random variable X has the probability density function given by

$$f(x) = \begin{cases} \frac{2}{3} + x^2 & 0 \le x \le 1 \\ 0 & \text{otherwise} \end{cases}$$

Find the value of $E(X)$.

3 The continuous random variable S has the probability density function given by

$$f(s) = \begin{cases} \frac{1}{18}\left(9 - s^2\right) & 0 \le s \le 3 \\ 0 & \text{otherwise} \end{cases}$$

Find the value of $E(S)$.

4 The continuous random variable T has the probability density function given by

$$f(t) = \begin{cases} kt^3 & 0 \le t \le 2 \\ 0 & \text{otherwise} \end{cases}$$

Find the value of   **(a)** k **(b)** $E(T)$

5 The continuous random variable X has the probability density function given by

$$f(x) = \begin{cases} \frac{1}{6}x & 0 \le x < 2 \\ \frac{1}{3} & 2 \le x < 4 \\ 0 & \text{otherwise} \end{cases}$$

(a) Sketch the graph of $f(x)$.   **(b)** Find $E(X)$.

6 The continuous random variable U has the probability density function given by

$$f(u) = \begin{cases} \frac{3}{5}u(2 - u) & 0 \le u < 1 \\ \frac{3}{5} & 1 \le u \le 2 \\ 0 & \text{otherwise} \end{cases}$$

(a) Sketch the graph of $f(u)$.   **(b)** Find $E(U)$.

7 The continuous random variable X has the probability density function given by

$$f(x) = \begin{cases} a - bx & 0 \le x \le 1 \\ 0 & \text{otherwise} \end{cases}$$

(a) By sketching the graph of $f(x)$, explain why $a \ge 0$ and why $a \ge b$.

(b) By considering the area under the graph of $f(x)$, explain why $a - \frac{1}{2}b = 1$.

(c) Given that $E(X) = \frac{3}{8}$, find another equation involving a and b.

(d) Solve the two equations to find the values of a and b.

E Expectation of a function of a continuous random variable (answers p 124)

In chapter 1 we looked at examples where a discrete random variable is defined as a function of a given random variable X, for example $\frac{1}{X}$.

The expectation of $\frac{1}{X}$ is found by multiplying each possible value of $\frac{1}{X}$ by its probability and then adding, so $E\left(\frac{1}{X}\right) = \sum \frac{1}{x_i} p_i$.

The corresponding expression for a continuous random variable X is

$$E\left(\frac{1}{X}\right) = \int \frac{1}{x} f(x)\, dx \quad \text{(with appropriate lower and upper limits of integration)}$$

E1 The continuous random variable X has the probability density function given by

$$f(x) = \begin{cases} \frac{1}{3}x^2 & 0 \le x \le 3 \\ 0 & \text{otherwise} \end{cases}$$

Show that $E\left(\frac{1}{X}\right) = \frac{3}{2}$.

Finding the expectation of other functions of X, such as X^2, X^3, X^{-2}, is similar.

> **K** If $g(X)$ is a function of X, then $E(g(X)) = \int g(x) f(x)\, dx$.
> For example, $E(X^3) = \int x^3 f(x)\, dx$.

E2 For the continuous random variable X defined in question E1, find
   (a) $E(X^2)$ (b) $E(X^3)$

In chapter 1 we saw that the expectation of a linear function $aX + b$ of a discrete random variable X is related in a simple way to the expectation of X. This also applies to a continuous random variable.

> **K** $E(aX + b) = aE(X) + b$

(The explanation is similar, with integration replacing summation.)

E3 For the continuous random variable X defined in question E1, find
   (a) $E(X)$ (b) $E(3X + 2)$ (c) $E\left(\frac{1}{2}X - 1\right)$

The rule $E(aX + b) = aE(X) + b$ applies to any continuous random variable. So it can be used for random variables that are functions of others. For example, if we have already found $E(X^3)$, then $E(2X^3 - 7) = 2E(X^3) - 7$.

E4 Use your answers to questions E1 and E2 to find
   (a) $E\left(\frac{3}{X} + 1\right)$ (b) $E(4X^2 - 3)$ (c) $E\left(20 - \frac{1}{5}X^3\right)$

Example 6

The continuous random variable T has the probability density function given by

$$f(t) = \begin{cases} \frac{3}{16}\left(4 - t^2\right) & 0 \le t \le 2 \\ 0 & \text{otherwise} \end{cases}$$

Find   (a) $\text{E}(T)$ (b) $\text{E}(3T + 1)$ (c) $\text{E}(T^3)$ (d) $\text{E}\left(\frac{1}{2}T^3 + 3\right)$

Solution

(a) $\text{E}(T) = \int t\,\text{f}(t)\,\text{d}t = \frac{3}{16}\int_0^2 t\left(4 - t^2\right)\text{d}t = \frac{3}{16}\int_0^2 \left(4t - t^3\right)\text{d}t = \frac{3}{16}\left[2t^2 - \frac{1}{4}t^4\right]_0^2 = \frac{3}{16}(8 - 4) = \frac{3}{4}$

(b) $\text{E}(3T + 1) = 3\text{E}(T) + 1 = \frac{9}{4} + 1 = 3\frac{1}{4}$

(c) $\text{E}\left(T^3\right) = \int t^3\,\text{f}(t)\,\text{d}t = \frac{3}{16}\int_0^2 t^3\left(4 - t^2\right)\text{d}t = \frac{3}{16}\int_0^2 \left(4t^3 - t^5\right)\text{d}t = \frac{3}{16}\left[t^4 - \frac{1}{6}t^6\right]_0^2 = \frac{3}{16}(16 - \frac{32}{3}) = 1$

(d) $\text{E}\left(\frac{1}{2}T^3 + 3\right) = \frac{1}{2}\text{E}(T^3) + 3 = \frac{1}{2} \times 1 + 3 = 3\frac{1}{2}$

Exercise E (answers p 124)

1 X is a continuous random variable such that $\text{E}(X) = 1.9$, $\text{E}(X^2) = 3.9$ and $\text{E}(X^{-1}) = 0.6$. Find

   (a) $\text{E}(5X - 2)$ (b) $\text{E}(3X^2 + 1)$ (c) $\text{E}(25 - 9X^{-1})$

2 The continuous random variable X has the probability density function given by

$$f(x) = \begin{cases} x + \frac{3}{2}x^2 & 0 \le x \le 1 \\ 0 & \text{otherwise} \end{cases}$$

Find

   (a) $\text{E}(X)$ (b) $\text{E}(3X - 1)$ (c) $\text{E}\left(\frac{1}{X}\right)$ (d) $\text{E}(X^2)$ (e) $\text{E}(X^3)$

3 The continuous random variable X has the probability density function given by

$$f(x) = \begin{cases} x + ax^3 & 0 \le x \le 2 \\ 0 & \text{otherwise} \end{cases}$$

   (a) By considering the area under the graph of $f(x)$, show that $a = -\frac{1}{4}$.

   (b) Find   (i) $\text{E}(X^2)$ (ii) $\text{E}(2X^2 + 5)$

   (c) Find   (i) $\text{E}\left(\frac{1}{X}\right)$ (ii) $\text{E}\left(\frac{3}{X} - 1\right)$

4 The continuous random variable T has the probability density function given by

$$f(t) = \begin{cases} k(t - 1)(7 - t) & 1 \le t \le 7 \\ 0 & \text{otherwise} \end{cases}$$

   (a) Find the value of k.

   (b) Find   (i) $\text{E}(T)$ (ii) $\text{E}(10 - T)$ (iii) $\text{E}(T^2)$

F Variance and standard deviation (answers p 125)

The definition of the variance of a continuous random variable corresponds to that of a discrete random variable.

Discrete random variable X: $\quad\quad \text{Var}(X) = \Sigma(x_i - \mu)^2 p_i$, where $\mu = \text{E}(X)$

Continuous random variable X: $\quad \text{Var}(X) = \int(x - \mu)^2 f(x)\, dx$ (with appropriate limits)

As in the discrete case, the definition is not the most convenient formula for calculating the variance. It is more convenient to use those shown below.

Discrete random variable X: $\quad\quad \text{Var}(X) = \Sigma x_i^2 p_i - \mu^2$

Continuous random variable X: $\quad \text{Var}(X) = \int x^2 f(x)\, dx - \mu^2$

Both of these formulae may be written in a way that is easy to remember:

K $\quad \text{Var}(X) = \text{E}(X^2) - [\text{E}(X)]^2$ 'variance = expectation of square – square of expectation'

The standard deviation σ is defined as $\sqrt{\text{Var}(X)}$.

F1 The continuous random variable X has the probability density function given by

$$f(x) = \begin{cases} \frac{1}{2}x & 0 \le x \le 2 \\ 0 & \text{otherwise} \end{cases}$$

$\text{E}(X) = \frac{4}{3}$.

(a) Find $\text{E}(X^2)$. $\quad\quad\quad\quad\quad\quad\quad\quad$ (b) Hence show that $\text{Var}(X) = \frac{2}{9}$.

F2 Find the variance of the continuous random variable X whose probability density function is given below. For this variable, $\text{E}(X) = \frac{9}{4}$.

$$f(x) = \begin{cases} \frac{1}{9}x^2 & 0 \le x \le 3 \\ 0 & \text{otherwise} \end{cases}$$

In chapter 1 we saw how the variance of a linear function of the discrete random variable $aX + b$ is related to the variance of X. The result also applies to continuous random variables.

K $\quad \text{Var}(aX + b) = a^2 \text{Var}(X)$

F3 The continuous random variable S has the probability density function given by

$$f(s) = \begin{cases} \frac{3}{8}s^2 & 0 \le s \le 2 \\ 0 & \text{otherwise} \end{cases}$$

Find the value of

(a) $\text{E}(S)$ $\quad\quad$ (b) $\text{E}(S^2)$ $\quad\quad$ (c) $\text{Var}(S)$ $\quad\quad$ (d) $\text{Var}(2S + 5)$ $\quad$ (e) $\text{Var}\left(\frac{1}{3}S - 1\right)$

F4 The continuous random variable T has the probability density function given by

$$f(t) = \begin{cases} 4t\left(1 - t^2\right) & 0 \le t \le 1 \\ 0 & \text{otherwise} \end{cases}$$

Find the value of

(a) $\text{E}(T)$ $\quad\quad\quad\quad$ (b) $\text{Var}(T)$ $\quad\quad\quad\quad$ (c) $\text{Var}(4T - 3)$ $\quad\quad\quad$ (d) $\text{Var}(8 - 3T)$

The formula $\mathrm{Var}(X) = \mathrm{E}(X^2) - [\mathrm{E}(X)]^2$ is also useful when you need to find the variance of a function of X, for example $\mathrm{Var}\left(\dfrac{1}{X}\right)$.

In the formula, you replace X by the function of X, so for example

$$\mathrm{Var}\left(\frac{1}{X}\right) = \mathrm{E}\left[\left(\frac{1}{X}\right)^2\right] - \left[\mathrm{E}\left(\frac{1}{X}\right)\right]^2$$

F5 The continuous random variable X has the probability density function given by

$$f(x) = \begin{cases} 4x^3 & 0 \le x \le 1 \\ 0 & \text{otherwise} \end{cases}$$

Find the value of

(a) $\mathrm{E}\left(\dfrac{1}{X}\right)$ (b) $\mathrm{E}\left(\dfrac{1}{X^2}\right)$ (c) $\mathrm{Var}\left(\dfrac{1}{X}\right)$

Example 7

The continuous random variable S has the probability density function given by

$$f(s) = \begin{cases} 12s^2(1-s) & 0 \le s \le 1 \\ 0 & \text{otherwise} \end{cases}$$

Find the value of (a) $\mathrm{Var}(S)$ (b) $\mathrm{Var}(5 - 3S)$ (c) $\mathrm{Var}(S^3)$

Solution

(a) Use the formula $\mathrm{Var}(S) = \mathrm{E}(S^2) - [\mathrm{E}(S)]^2$.

$$\mathrm{E}(S) = \int_0^1 s \times 12s^2(1-s)\,ds = 12\int_0^1 (s^3 - s^4)\,ds = 12\left[\tfrac{1}{4}s^4 - \tfrac{1}{5}s^5\right]_0^1 = 12\left(\tfrac{1}{4} - \tfrac{1}{5}\right) = \tfrac{3}{5}$$

$$\mathrm{E}(S^2) = \int_0^1 s^2 \times 12s^2(1-s)\,ds = 12\int_0^1 (s^4 - s^5)\,ds = 12\left[\tfrac{1}{5}s^5 - \tfrac{1}{6}s^6\right]_0^1 = 12\left(\tfrac{1}{5} - \tfrac{1}{6}\right) = \tfrac{2}{5}$$

So $\mathrm{Var}(S) = \tfrac{2}{5} - \left(\tfrac{3}{5}\right)^2 = \tfrac{2}{5} - \tfrac{9}{25} = \tfrac{10}{25} - \tfrac{9}{25} = \tfrac{1}{25}$

(b) $\mathrm{Var}(5 - 3S) = \mathrm{Var}(-3S + 5) = (-3)^2 \times \mathrm{Var}(S) = 9 \times \tfrac{1}{25} = \tfrac{9}{25}$

(c) Use the formula in (a), but with S^3 replacing S: $\mathrm{Var}(S^3) = \mathrm{E}[(S^3)^2] - [\mathrm{E}(S^3)]^2$
$$= \mathrm{E}(S^6) - [\mathrm{E}(S^3)]^2$$

$$\mathrm{E}(S^3) = \int_0^1 s^3 \times 12s^2(1-s)\,ds = 12\int_0^1 (s^5 - s^6)\,ds = 12\left[\tfrac{1}{6}s^6 - \tfrac{1}{7}s^7\right]_0^1 = 12\left(\tfrac{1}{6} - \tfrac{1}{7}\right) = \tfrac{2}{7}$$

$$\mathrm{E}(S^6) = \int_0^1 s^6 \times 12s^2(1-s)\,ds = 12\int_0^1 (s^8 - s^9)\,ds = 12\left[\tfrac{1}{9}s^9 - \tfrac{1}{10}s^{10}\right]_0^1 = 12\left(\tfrac{1}{9} - \tfrac{1}{10}\right) = \tfrac{2}{15}$$

So $\mathrm{Var}(S^3) = \tfrac{2}{15} - \left(\tfrac{2}{7}\right)^2 = \tfrac{2}{15} - \tfrac{4}{49} = \tfrac{38}{735}$

1 The continuous random variable X has the probability density function given by

$$f(x) = \begin{cases} k(x+2) & 0 \le x \le 4 \\ 0 & \text{otherwise} \end{cases}$$

(a) Find the value of k.

(b) Find   **(i)** $E(X)$ **(ii)** $E(X^2)$ **(iii)** $\text{Var}(X)$ **(iv)** $\text{Var}(2X-1)$

2 The continuous random variable X has the probability density function given by

$$f(x) = \begin{cases} x - \frac{3}{8}x^2 & 0 \le x \le 2 \\ 0 & \text{otherwise} \end{cases}$$

Find

(a) $E(X)$ **(b)** $E(X^2)$ **(c)** $\text{Var}(X)$ **(d)** $\text{Var}(10-X)$

3 The continuous random variable X has the probability density function given by

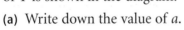

$$f(x) = \begin{cases} \frac{3}{64}x^2 & 0 \le x \le 4 \\ 0 & \text{otherwise} \end{cases}$$

(a) Find   **(i)** $E(X)$ **(ii)** $E(X^2)$ **(iii)** $\text{Var}(X)$

(b) Find   **(i)** $E\left(\dfrac{1}{X}\right)$ **(ii)** $E\left(\dfrac{1}{X^2}\right)$ **(iii)** $\text{Var}\left(\dfrac{1}{X}\right)$

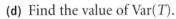

4 The continuous random variable U has the probability density function given by

$$f(u) = \begin{cases} \frac{1}{24}(8-u) & 0 \le u \le 4 \\ 0 & \text{otherwise} \end{cases}$$

(a) Find   **(i)** $E(U)$ **(ii)** $\text{Var}(U)$

(b) Find   **(i)** $E(U^3)$ **(ii)** $\text{Var}(U^3)$

5 An alarm is set to go off at some time during the interval from 12:00 to 12:08. The time, in minutes after 12:00, at which the alarm sounds is modelled by the continuous random variable T.

The graph of the probability density function of T is shown in the diagram.

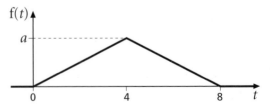

(a) Write down the value of a.

(b) Find the equation of each part of the probability density function.

(c) Explain, without doing any calculation, why $E(T) = 4$.

(d) Find the value of $\text{Var}(T)$.

(e) Given that the standard deviation of T is σ, find the probability that T lies in the interval from $4 - \sigma$ to $4 + \sigma$. Give your answer to 3 s.f.

G Rectangular distribution (answers p 125)

A discrete random variable has a uniform distribution if the probabilities of all the possible values are equal. For example, the score on an ordinary dice has a uniform distribution.

The corresponding distribution for a continuous random variable is called a **rectangular** distribution.

The diagram shows the rectangular distribution on the interval 0 to 5.

To make the area under the graph equal to 1, the height has to be $\frac{1}{5}$, so the probability density function is given by

$$f(x) = \begin{cases} \frac{1}{5} & 0 \le x \le 5 \\ 0 & \text{otherwise} \end{cases}$$

K In general, the probability density function of the rectangular distribution on the interval from a to b is given by

$$f(x) = \begin{cases} \dfrac{1}{b-a} & a \le x \le b \\ 0 & \text{otherwise} \end{cases}$$

G1 A continuous random variable X has the rectangular distribution on the interval from 2 to 6, as shown in the diagram.

(a) What is the value of k?

(b) Find $P(2 \le X \le 3.5)$.

(c) Without doing any calculations, state the mean or expected value of X.

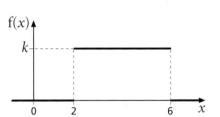

The diagram shows the rectangular distribution on the interval from 0 to l. The probability density function is given by

$$f(x) = \begin{cases} \dfrac{1}{l} & 0 \le x \le l \\ 0 & \text{otherwise} \end{cases}$$

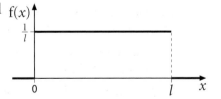

The expected value $E(X) = \int_0^l x\,\frac{1}{l}\,dx = \frac{1}{l}\left[\frac{x^2}{2}\right]_0^l = \frac{l^2}{2l} = \frac{l}{2}$.

This is not surprising as the distribution is symmetrical about the value $\dfrac{l}{2}$.

$$\text{Var}(X) = E(X^2) - [E(X)]^2 = \int_0^l x^2\,\frac{1}{l}\,dx - \left(\frac{l}{2}\right)^2 = \frac{1}{l}\int_0^l x^2\,dx - \frac{l^2}{4}$$

$$= \frac{1}{l}\left[\frac{x^3}{3}\right]_0^l - \frac{l^2}{4} = \frac{l^3}{3l} - \frac{l^2}{4} = l^2\left(\frac{1}{3} - \frac{1}{4}\right) = \frac{l^2}{12}$$

These results can be written

$$E(X) = \text{mid-interval value} \qquad \text{Var}(X) = \frac{(\text{length of interval})^2}{12}$$

The two results obtained on the previous page apply to any rectangular distribution, because if the entire distribution on the interval 0 to l is shifted along the axis, the mean value will still be halfway along the interval and the variance will be unchanged.

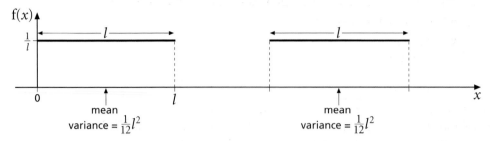

G2 Show that the standard deviation of the rectangular distribution on an interval of length l is $\dfrac{l}{2\sqrt{3}}$.

K If X has the rectangular distribution on an interval of length l, then
$E(X)$ is at the mid-point of the interval and $Var(X) = \dfrac{l^2}{12}$.

Example 8

The weight in grams of a burger produced by a machine is modelled as a continuous random variable W with the rectangular distribution on the interval from 220 to 280.

(a) Find

    (i) $E(W)$ (ii) $Var(W)$ (iii) the standard deviation of W

(b) Find the probability that a burger produced by the machine weighs within one standard deviation either side of the mean weight.

Solution

This is the graph of the probability density function.
The interval is of length 60, so the height of the graph is $\frac{1}{60}$.

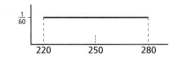

(a) (i) $E(W) =$ mid-point of interval from 220 to 280 $= 250$

    (ii) $Var(W) = \frac{1}{12}$(length of interval)$^2 = \frac{1}{12} \times 60^2 = 300$

    (iii) Standard deviation $= \sqrt{300} = 17.32$ (to 2 d.p.)

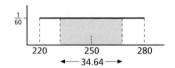

(b) The length of the interval from (mean $- \sigma$) to (mean $+ \sigma$)
$= 2\sigma = 34.64$.
The probability for an interval of length $34.64 = \frac{1}{60} \times 34.64$
$$= 0.577 \text{ (to 3 s.f.)}$$

Exercise G (answers p 125)

   1 The error, X volts, in the reading on a voltmeter has the rectangular distribution on the interval $-0.3 \le x \le 0.3$.

   State the value of the mean of X and find the variance and standard deviation of X.

2 The continuous random variable X has the rectangular distribution on the interval $1 \le x \le 9$. Find $P(2.5 \le X \le 4)$.

3 The continuous random variable X has the rectangular distribution with probability density function given by

$$f(x) = \begin{cases} k & 1 \le x \le 7 \\ 0 & \text{otherwise} \end{cases}$$

(a) Find the value of k.   **(b)** Find $P(1 \le X \le 4)$.

(c) State the value of $E(X)$ and prove that $Var(X) = 3$.
('Prove' means that you cannot use the result 'variance = length^2/12'. You must find the variance using $Var(X) = E(X^2) - [E(X)]^2$.)

(d) Find the value of   **(i)** $E(3X - 1)$ **(ii)** $Var(3X - 1)$

4 The continuous random variable T has the rectangular distribution with probability density function given by

$$f(t) = \begin{cases} 0.05 & 5 \le t \le h \\ 0 & \text{otherwise} \end{cases}$$

(a) Find the value of h.   **(b)** Find $P(10 \le T \le 12)$.

(c) Find $E(T)$.   **(d)** Find $Var(T)$.

Key points

- If $f(x)$ is the probability density function of the continuous random variable X, then

  $$\int_{-\infty}^{\infty} f(x)\,dx = 1 \qquad P(a \le X \le b) = \int_{a}^{b} f(x)\,dx \qquad P(X = a) = 0 \qquad \text{(p 40)}$$

- The distribution function $F(x)$ is defined by $F(x) = P(X < x)$.   (p 43)

- $f(x) = F'(x)$ or $f(x) = \dfrac{d}{dx}F(x)$ (p 44)

- $P(X < \text{median}) = \frac{1}{2}$ $P(X < \text{lower quartile}) = \frac{1}{4}$ $P(X < \text{upper quartile}) = \frac{3}{4}$
  $P(X < \text{20th percentile}) = 0.20$, etc.   (p 45)

- $E(X) = \int x f(x)\,dx$ (with appropriate limits)   (p 50)

- If $g(X)$ is a function of X, then $E(g(X)) = \int g(x) f(x)\,dx$ (p 52)

- $E(aX + b) = aE(X) + b$ (p 52)

- $Var(X) = E(X^2) - [E(X)]^2$ 'variance = expectation of square – square of expectation' (p 54)

- $Var(aX + b) = a^2 Var(X)$ (p 54)

- For the rectangular distribution on the interval (a, b), $f(x) = \begin{cases} \dfrac{1}{b-a} & a \le x \le b \\ 0 & \text{otherwise} \end{cases}$

  The mean is $\frac{1}{2}(a + b)$ and the variance $\frac{1}{12}(b - a)^2$.

  (pp 57, 58)

Mixed questions (answers p 126)

1 The continuous random variable X has the probability density function given by

$$f(x) = \begin{cases} kx(x-2)^2 & 0 \le x \le 2 \\ 0 & \text{otherwise} \end{cases}$$

(a) Show that $k = \frac{3}{4}$.   **(b)** Find $P(X > 1)$.   **(c)** Find $E(X)$.

2 The continuous random variable X has the probability density function given by

$$f(x) = \begin{cases} kx^3 & 0 \le x \le 4 \\ 0 & \text{otherwise} \end{cases}$$

(a) Find the value of k.   **(b)** Find the median of X.   **(c)** Find the 80th percentile of X.

3 In a traffic study, the time interval in minutes between vehicles passing a point on a road is modelled as a continuous random variable T with the following probability density function.

$$f(t) = \begin{cases} k(t-3)^2 & 0 \le t \le 3 \\ 0 & \text{otherwise} \end{cases}$$

(a) Show that $k = \frac{1}{9}$.

(b) Find the probability that the interval between vehicles is longer than 2 minutes.

(c) Find the mean interval between vehicles.

(d) Find the standard deviation of the interval between vehicles.

4 The continuous random variable T has the probability density function given by

$$f(t) = \begin{cases} k(2t+3) & 0 \le t \le 3 \\ 0 & \text{otherwise} \end{cases}$$

(a) Sketch the graph of f.

(b) Find the value of k.

(c) Show that the distribution function of T is $F(t) = \frac{1}{18}t(t+3)$.

(d) Show that if m is the median value of T, then $m^2 + 3m - 9 = 0$ and hence find the value of m to three significant figures.

(e) Find   **(i)** $E(T)$ **(ii)** $\text{Var}(T)$ **(iii)** $E(8-2T)$ **(iv)** $\text{Var}(8-2T)$

(f) Find   **(i)** $E(T^3)$ **(ii)** $\text{Var}(T^3)$ **(iii)** $E(2T^3+1)$ **(iv)** $\text{Var}(2T^3+1)$

5 The error made by a student reading from a scale is modelled as a continuous random variable with the rectangular distribution on the interval -0.5 to 0.5. Find the standard deviation of the error, correct to three significant figures.

6 The continuous random variable S has the probability density function given by

$$f(s) = \begin{cases} \frac{3}{4}s^2(2-s) & 0 \le s \le 2 \\ 0 & \text{otherwise} \end{cases}$$

Find   **(a)** $E(S^{-1})$ **(b)** $\text{Var}(S^{-1})$

Test yourself (answers p 126)

1 At a Post Office, the time, T minutes, that customers have to wait in order to be served has the following probability density function.

$$f(t) = \begin{cases} \dfrac{t^2}{18} & 0 \le t \le 3 \\ \frac{1}{4}(5-t) & 3 \le t \le 5 \\ 0 & \text{otherwise} \end{cases}$$

(a) Write down the value of $P(T=4)$.

(b) Show that the median waiting time is 3 minutes.

(c) Find the probability that customers have to wait for less than 3.5 minutes to be served.

(d) Calculate the mean time that customers have to wait in order to be served.   AQA 2003

2 The continuous random variable X has the rectangular distribution with the following probability density function.

$$f(x) = \begin{cases} k & a \le x \le a+5 \\ 0 & \text{otherwise} \end{cases}$$

(a) Find the value of k.

(b) Find $P(X > a+1)$.

(c) Find $E(X)$ in terms of a.

(d) Find the value of   (i) $\text{Var}(X)$ (ii) $\text{Var}(5X-4)$

3 The continuous random variable X has the following probability density function.

$$f(x) = \begin{cases} kx & 0 \le x \le 4 \\ 0 & \text{otherwise} \end{cases}$$

(a) Show that the value of the constant k is $\frac{1}{8}$.

(b) Given that $E(X) = 2\frac{2}{3}$, calculate the variance of X.

(c) Hence calculate $\text{Var}(5X-4)$.

(d) Calculate the 90th percentile of X.   AQA 2002

4 The continuous random variable X has the probability density function given by

$$f(x) = \begin{cases} \frac{3}{40}x(4-x) & 0 \le x \le 2 \\ \frac{3}{10} & 2 \le x \le 4 \\ 0 & \text{otherwise} \end{cases}$$

(a) Sketch the graph of f.

(b) Find $P(X < 3)$.

(c) Find   (i) $E(X)$ (ii) $\text{Var}(X)$

(d) Find   (i) $E\left(\dfrac{1}{X}\right)$ (ii) $E\left(\dfrac{1}{3X}+2\right)$

4 Estimation

In this chapter you will learn how to find confidence intervals for the mean of a normal distribution with unknown variance.

A Normal distribution: review

The normal distribution is an example of a continuous distribution.

If Z is a continuous random variable with the standard normal distribution, the probability density function of Z is given by $f(z) = \dfrac{1}{\sqrt{2\pi}} e^{-\frac{1}{2}z^2}$.

For this distribution $E(Z) = 0$ and $Var(Z) = 1$.

The formula for $f(z)$ is seldom used in practice, because areas under the graph of $f(z)$ can be found from tables (or some calculators).

The value of $P(Z < z)$ is denoted by $\Phi(z)$. (So $\Phi(z)$ is the distribution function of Z.)

<table>
<tr>
<td>

The standard normal distribution table (on page 112) gives values of $\Phi(z)$, the area under the graph to the left of z.

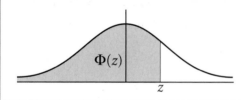

</td>
<td>

The percentage points table (on page 113) shows, for a given probability p, the value of z for which $\Phi(z) = p$.

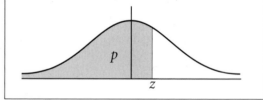

</td>
</tr>
</table>

If X is a continuous random variable with the general normal distribution with mean μ and variance σ^2, then the variable Z given by $Z = \dfrac{X - \mu}{\sigma}$ has mean 0 and variance 1. The variable Z is the **standardised variable** corresponding to X.

Probabilities relating to X can be found from the standard normal table by using values of the standardised variable Z.

Example 1

The continuous random variable X is normally distributed with mean 20 and variance 16.

(a) Find $P(X < 15)$.   **(b)** Find the value of k for which $P(20 - k < X < 20 + k) = 0.95$.

Solution

(a) $\sigma = \sqrt{16} = 4$. Let $Z = \dfrac{X - \mu}{\sigma} = \dfrac{X - 20}{4}$.

When $X = 15$, $Z = \dfrac{15 - 20}{4} = -1.25$, so $P(X < 15) = P(Z < -1.25)$.

$P(Z < -1.25)$ is this area: 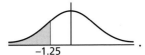 .

The table of $\Phi(z)$ gives values for positive values of z.
For negative z we use the symmetry of the graph.

The area above is found by subtracting the area shown here from 1.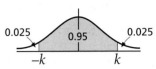

So, using the table of $\Phi(z)$, $P(Z < -1.25) = 1 - \Phi(1.25) = 1 - 0.894\,35 = 0.105\,65$.

(b) The interval $20 - k < X < 20 + k$ corresponds to an interval of the form $-k < Z < k$.

The situation is as shown in the diagram on the right.

So k is the value of z for which $\Phi(z) = 1 - 0.025 = 0.975$.

From the percentage points table, $k = 1.9600$.

This standardised value has to be converted into a corresponding value of X.

This can be done by rearranging the equation $Z = \dfrac{X - 20}{4}$ as $X = 4Z + 20$.

So when $Z = 1.9600$, $X = 4 \times 1.9600 + 20 = 27.84$. So $k = 7.84$ (to 2 d.p.).

Exercise A (answers p 127)

1 The random variable X is normally distributed with mean 10 and standard deviation 2.5.

(a) Express Z, the standard normal variable corresponding to X, in terms of X.

(b) (i) State the value of Z corresponding to $X = 14$.

(ii) Find $P(X < 14)$.

(c) Find   (i) $P(11 \le X \le 12)$ (ii) $P(8 \le X \le 14)$ (iii) $P(X > 7)$

(d) (i) Find the value of a such that $P(Z < a) = 0.8$.

(ii) Hence find the value of b such that $P(X < b) = 0.8$.

(e) Find the value of b such that

(i) $P(X < b) = 0.95$ (ii) $P(10 - b < X < 10 + b) = 0.9$

2 The volume of liquid poured into a bottle of FiziCola at the factory is normally distributed with mean 126 ml and standard deviation 1.6 ml. Bottles that contain less than 124 ml or more than 130 ml are rejected. What is the probability that a bottle will be rejected?

3 A machine can be set to produce burgers of a given mean weight. The weights of burgers produced by the machine are normally distributed about this mean with standard deviation 6 g. To what value should the mean be set if the percentage of burgers weighing less than 220 g is to be no more than 4%?

4 The random variable X is normally distributed with mean 140 and standard deviation σ.

(a) Find the value of σ given that $P(X < 177.6) = 0.88$.

(b) Find the value of a given that $P(X < a) = 0.34$.

B Unbiased estimators and estimates: review

Estimating μ

Suppose that the weights of a large colony of seals are distributed with mean μ and variance σ^2. The distribution is not necessarily normal.

A common procedure in statistics is to try to get information about the population as a whole by taking a random sample.

The weight of a seal picked at random from the colony is a continuous random variable with mean μ and variance σ^2.

If a random sample of n seals is to be selected, the weight of each seal in the sample will be independent of each of the others. Each of the n weights is a continuous random variable with the same distribution with mean μ and variance σ^2.

Let these n independent random variables be $X_1, X_2, X_3, \ldots, X_n$.

The random variable $\overline{X}$ given by $\overline{X} = \dfrac{X_1 + X_2 + \ldots + X_n}{n}$ is called the **sample mean**. It can be shown that the expected value of $\overline{X}$ is also μ.

We say that the sample mean $\overline{X}$ is an **unbiased estimator** of the population mean μ, because its expected value, or mean, is equal to μ: $E(\overline{X}) = \mu$.

Suppose that a particular sample is taken and the recorded values are $x_1, x_2, \ldots, x_n$. The mean of these recorded values, $\bar{x}$, is an **unbiased estimate** of μ.

The word 'estimator' and the capital letter $\overline{X}$ are used for the random variable. This is when we are thinking of the sample mean $\overline{X}$ as a quantity that can take a range of possible values and that has a probability distribution.

We use the lower-case letter $\bar{x}$ to denote the particular value of $\overline{X}$ that we get from an actual sample. The value $\bar{x}$ is an unbiased estimate of μ obtained from this sample.

Estimating σ^2

It can be shown that the random variable S^2, defined by

$$S^2 = \frac{\left(X_1 - \overline{X}\right)^2 + \left(X_2 - \overline{X}\right)^2 + \ldots + \left(X_n - \overline{X}\right)^2}{n-1}$$

is an unbiased estimator of the population variance σ^2. (For a proof, see page 75.)

Notice that the denominator in the definition of S^2 is $n - 1$, not n. The number $n - 1$ is called the number of **degrees of freedom** in the definition of S^2.

The n variables in the numerator, $(X_1 - \overline{X})^2$, $(X_2 - \overline{X})^2$, ... are not totally independent of one another, because

$$(X_1 - \overline{X}) + (X_2 - \overline{X}) + \ldots + (X_n - \overline{X}) = \Sigma X_i - n\overline{X} = \Sigma X_i - n\frac{\Sigma X_i}{n} = 0$$

There are only $n - 1$ independent variables in the definition, hence only $n - 1$ degrees of freedom.

As before, we use the capital letter S^2 for the estimator and the lower-case letter s^2 for the particular value of S^2 obtained from a sample.

$$s^2 = \frac{(x_1 - \bar{x})^2 + (x_2 - \bar{x})^2 + \ldots + (x_n - \bar{x})^2}{n-1}$$

The numerator of this expression is more easily calculated as $\sum x_i^2 - n\bar{x}^2$, so

$$s^2 = \frac{\sum x_i^2 - n\bar{x}^2}{n-1}$$

Most scientific calculators have a key labelled σ_{n-1} or s_{n-1}. Using this key will give the value of s for a sample. To find s^2, the unbiased estimate of the variance, you need to square the value obtained from the calculator.

Note: S^2 is an unbiased estimator of the variance σ^2, but S is **not** an unbiased estimator of the standard deviation σ. This is because the expected value of the square root of a variable is not equal to the square root of the expected value.

Example 2

A random sample of 15 tomatoes of a certain variety was taken. The weights, in grams, of the tomatoes were

   67   58   55   69   71   52   55   58   70   63   51   66   68   64   60

Find unbiased estimates for the mean and variance of the weights of tomatoes of this variety.

Solution

$$\bar{x} = \frac{\sum x_i}{n} = \frac{67 + 58 + 55 + \ldots + 60}{15} = 61.8$$

$$s^2 = \frac{\sum x_i^2 - n\bar{x}^2}{n-1} = \frac{67^2 + 58^2 + \ldots + 60^2 - 15 \times 61.8^2}{14} = 45.028\ldots$$

These results can be found by using the statistics mode on a calculator.
After entering the data, use the $\bar{x}$ and σ_{n-1} keys, but square the latter result.

Unbiased estimates are, to 3 s.f., mean: 61.8, variance: 45.0.

Exercise B (answers p 127)

1 In order to estimate the fuel economy of a model of car, ten cars were selected at random and the fuel economy, in litres per 100 km, of each car was measured. The results were: 10.5 11.3 10.9 10.2 11.8 11.9 12.4 10.1 12.2 12.0

   Find unbiased estimates of the mean and variance of the fuel economy of the model.

2 At an early stage in the marking of an exam, the examiners want estimates of the mean mark and the variance. The papers of a random sample of 20 candidates are marked. For these papers, $\sum x_i = 876$ and $\sum x_i^2 = 42\,078$.

   Find unbiased estimates of the mean and variance of the marks in the exam.

C Sampling distribution: review

The distribution of the weights of adult animals of a certain species is often closely approximated by a normal distribution.

Suppose that the weights in kilograms of a large colony of seals are normally distributed with mean 20 and variance 22.5. A random sample of 10 seals is to be taken.

In this case, where the distribution is normal, it can be shown that the sample mean also has a normal distribution with the same mean, 20, but with variance $\frac{1}{10}$ of that of the population.

The general result is as follows:

Suppose that $X_1, X_2, X_3, \ldots X_n$ are n independent random variables, each normally distributed with mean μ and variance σ^2, and that $\overline{X} = \dfrac{\Sigma X_i}{n}$.

Then $\overline{X}$ is also normally distributed, with mean μ and variance $\dfrac{\sigma^2}{n}$.   (1)

The distribution of $\overline{X}$ is called the **sampling distribution of the sample mean**.

The standard deviation of $\overline{X}$ is called the **standard error of the sample mean**.

Its value is $\sqrt{\dfrac{\sigma^2}{n}} = \dfrac{\sigma}{\sqrt{n}}$.

'Standard error' is not a good description, but it is useful to have a way of distinguishing between the standard deviation of the population and the standard deviation of the sample mean.

If X stands for the weight of a seal chosen at random from the population described above, then X is normally distributed with mean 20 and variance 22.5. This may be written as $X \sim N(20, 22.5)$.

If $\overline{X}$ is the mean of a sample of size 10, then $\overline{X}$ is normally distributed with mean 20 and variance $\frac{22.5}{10} = 2.25$. The standard error in this case is $\sqrt{2.25} = 1.5$.

The distributions of X and $\overline{X}$ are shown below.

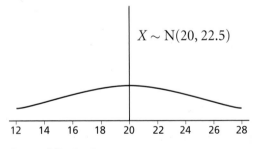

$X \sim N(20, 22.5)$

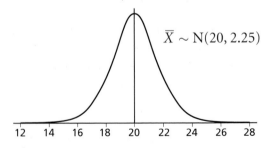

$\overline{X} \sim N(20, 2.25)$

Central limit theorem

It can be shown that statement (1) above remains true even if the distribution of each of the variables $X_1, X_2, \ldots$ is not normal, provided that

(1) all the variables $X_1, X_2, \ldots$ have the same distribution, with mean μ and variance σ^2

(2) the value of n is sufficiently large ($n \geq 30$)

Example 3

The weights in kilograms of a species of fish in a lake are normally distributed with mean 3.5 and variance 0.625.
A random sample of 10 fish of the species is taken from the lake.
Find the probability that the mean weight of the sample is greater than 4 kg.

Solution

The mean weight W of a sample of size 10 is normally distributed with mean 3.5 and variance $\frac{0.625}{10} = 0.0625$.

So the standard deviation of W is $\sqrt{0.0625} = 0.25$.

The standardised variable corresponding to W is $Z = \dfrac{W - 3.5}{0.25}$.

When $W = 4$, $Z = \dfrac{4 - 3.5}{0.25} = 2$.

So $P(W > 4) = P(Z > 2) = 1 - P(Z < 2) = 1 - \Phi(2) = 1 - 0.977\,25 = 0.022\,75$

Example 4

The lifetime of a type of light bulb is distributed with mean 2800 hours and standard deviation 180 hours. Find the probability that the mean lifetime of a random sample of 40 bulbs is less than 2750 hours.

Solution

As the sample size is greater than 30, by the central limit theorem the distribution of the sample mean $\bar{X}$ can be treated as a normal distribution.

So $\bar{X}$ is normally distributed with mean 2800 and standard deviation $\dfrac{180}{\sqrt{40}} = 28.46$.

The standardised variable corresponding to $\bar{X}$ is $Z = \dfrac{\bar{X} - 2800}{28.46}$. When $X = 2750$, $Z = -1.76$.

So $P(\bar{X} < 2750) = P(Z < -1.76) = 1 - P(Z < 1.76) = 1 - 0.96080 = 0.0392$

Exercise C (answers p 127)

1 The lifetimes of a type of battery are normally distributed with mean 400 hours and standard deviation 16 hours. The random variable $\bar{X}$ is the mean lifetime of a random sample of 25 batteries.

   (a) Find $P(\bar{X} \le 402)$.

   (b) Find the value of k for which $P(400 - k < \bar{X} < 400 + k) = 0.95$.

2 The mean weight of a species of fish is 258.0 g and the standard deviation of the weights is 11.4 g. Apart from this, nothing is known about the distribution.

   A random sample of 36 fish is to be taken. Find an approximation to the probability that the mean of the sample is greater than 255.0 g, explaining why your method is appropriate.

D Confidence intervals: review

Suppose the weight X kg of a fish taken at random from a lake is normally distributed with unknown mean μ and variance known to be 1.8.

A sample of 20 fish will be taken. We know in advance that the mean weight $\overline{X}$ of the sample is normally distributed with mean μ and variance $\frac{1.8}{20} = 0.09$.

The standard error of $\overline{X}$ is $\sqrt{0.09} = 0.3$.

The distribution of $\overline{X}$ is shown in this diagram. The second scale below the axis shows the standardised variable $Z = \dfrac{\overline{X} - \mu}{0.3}$.

From the percentage points table, $P(Z < 1.96) = 0.975$, so $P(-1.96 < Z < 1.96) = 0.95$.

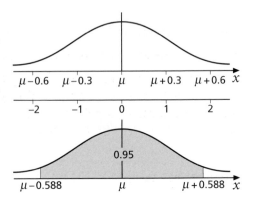

To convert this into a statement about $\overline{X}$, we need to express $\overline{X}$ in terms of Z: $\overline{X} = \mu + 0.3Z$

When $Z = -1.96$, $\overline{X} = \mu - 0.3 \times 1.96 = \mu - 0.588$

When $Z = 1.96$, $\overline{X} = \mu + 0.3 \times 1.96 = \mu + 0.588$

So there is a probability of 95% that the value of the sample mean will be in the interval from $\mu - 0.588$ to $\mu + 0.588$, as shown in the diagram above.

Suppose now a sample of 20 fish is taken and that the mean weight is 4.320 kg. We ask: 'What values of μ would make this result likely?'

If the population mean μ were, say 3 kg, then the interval from $\mu - 0.588$ to $\mu + 0.588$ would be from $3 - 0.588$ to $3 + 0.588$, or 2.412 to 3.588. This would make a recorded result of 4.320 very unlikely.

Similarly, if μ were 6 kg, the interval would be from $6 - 0.588$ to $6 + 0.588$, or 5.412 to 6.588. This too would make the recorded result 4.320 very unlikely.

These two situations are shown in the diagram below.

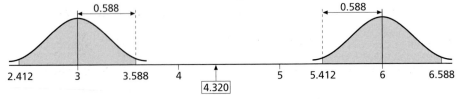

The two limiting cases, where the result 4.320 is on the boundary of being unlikely, are shown below.

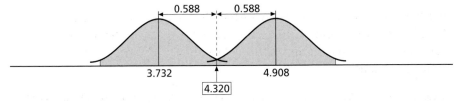

The interval from $4.320 - 0.588$ to $4.320 + 0.588$, or 3.732 to 4.908, is called the 95% **confidence interval** for μ.

Giving a 95% confidence interval is a way of stating an estimate of an unknown parameter of a distribution, in this case μ, based on the results of a sample.

If the recorded values in the sample are called $x_1, x_2, x_3, \ldots$ then the recorded value of the mean of the sample is $\bar{x} = \dfrac{\Sigma x_i}{n}$.

If the population variance σ^2 is known, the standard deviation of the random variable $\bar{X}$ is $\dfrac{\sigma}{\sqrt{n}}$.

The 95% confidence interval for μ is from $\bar{x} - 1.96\left(\dfrac{\sigma}{\sqrt{n}}\right)$ to $\bar{x} + 1.96\left(\dfrac{\sigma}{\sqrt{n}}\right)$.

Other confidence intervals can also be defined.

For example, the percentage points table tells us that $P(Z < 1.6449) = 0.95$, so the probability is 0.90 that a standard normal variable Z will lie in the interval from -1.6449 to 1.6449. (See diagram.)

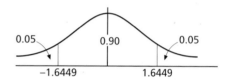

The corresponding 90% confidence interval for μ is $\bar{x} - 1.6449\left(\dfrac{\sigma}{\sqrt{n}}\right)$ to $\bar{x} + 1.6449\left(\dfrac{\sigma}{\sqrt{n}}\right)$.

The 90% confidence interval is narrower than the 95% interval, which is what we would expect as we are less confident that it contains the value of μ.

Example 5

The quantity of jam put into a jar by a machine, when working properly, is normally distributed with mean 500 g and standard deviation 8 g. After a breakdown, a random sample of 10 jars is taken and a sample mean of 494 g is recorded. Assuming that the standard deviation has not changed, construct a 95% confidence interval for the new mean quantity the machine puts into a jar.

Solution

The standard error of the sample mean $= \dfrac{8}{\sqrt{10}}$. The recorded sample mean $\bar{x} = 494$.

For a 95% confidence interval, we need the 97.5% percentage point, which is 1.96.

The interval is from $494 - 1.96 \times \dfrac{8}{\sqrt{10}}$ to $494 + 1.96 \times \dfrac{8}{\sqrt{10}}$, or from 489.04 to 498.96.

Exercise D (answers p 127)

1 The length of a species of snake is normally distributed with unknown mean but with standard deviation 16 cm. A random sample of 20 snakes yielded a recorded sample mean of 155 cm. Construct a 95% confidence interval for the mean length of the species.

2 The standard deviation of the diameter of pebbles on a beach is known to be 16 mm. A random sample of 100 pebbles was found to have a mean diameter of 48 mm. Construct a 90% confidence interval for the mean diameter of pebbles on this beach, explaining why you can assume that the sample mean is normally distributed.

E Confidence intervals: variance unknown (answers p 127)

Suppose that $X_1, X_2, X_3, \ldots, X_n$ are n independent random variables, each normally distributed with mean μ and variance σ^2.

We have seen that the random variable $\overline{X} = \dfrac{\Sigma X_i}{n}$ is also normally distributed, with mean μ and variance $\dfrac{\sigma^2}{n}$.

The standardised variable corresponding to $\overline{X}$ is $Z = \dfrac{\overline{X} - \mu}{\left(\dfrac{\sigma}{\sqrt{n}}\right)}$, and this has the standard normal distribution.

By using the percentage points of the distribution of Z, we are able to construct confidence intervals for μ. For example, a 95% confidence interval for μ is

$$\text{from } \bar{x} - 1.96\left(\frac{\sigma}{\sqrt{n}}\right) \text{ to } \bar{x} + 1.96\left(\frac{\sigma}{\sqrt{n}}\right)$$

But this method works only if the population variance σ^2 is known. We shall now look at the situation where the value of σ^2 is unknown, which is far more common in practice.

We saw in section B that it is possible to use the sample itself to give an estimate of σ^2.

The random variable S^2, defined by $S^2 = \dfrac{(X_1 - \overline{X})^2 + (X_2 - \overline{X})^2 + \ldots + (X_n - \overline{X})^2}{n-1}$,

is an unbiased estimator of the population variance σ^2.

t-distribution

If the σ in the standardised variable for $\overline{X}$ is replaced by S, the variable becomes $\dfrac{\overline{X} - \mu}{\left(\dfrac{S}{\sqrt{n}}\right)}$.

The British chemist and statistician William Sealey Gosset (1876–1937) showed that this random variable does not have the standard normal distribution, but a different type of distribution.

This type of distribution is called a **t-distribution**. The actual distribution depends on the number of degrees of freedom in the definition of S^2, which is $n-1$.

This diagram shows some t-distributions with different numbers of degrees of freedom (d.f.), together with the standard normal distribution for comparison.

As the number of degrees of freedom increases, the t-distribution gets closer and closer to the normal distribution.

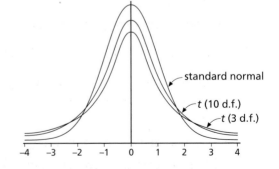

Gosset, who worked for Guinness in Dublin, investigated how barley yields could be improved, and this involved drawing conclusions from samples. He wrote under the pen name 'Student', so the t-distribution is often called 'Student's t-distribution'.

The table of percentage points of the *t*-distribution is on page 114. Here is part of it.

The number of degrees of freedom is shown as v ('nu', the Greek letter n).

The table shows, for each value of p, the value of x for which $P(X \leq x) = p$, where X is a random variable having the *t*-distribution with v degrees of freedom.

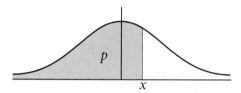

p	0.9	0.95	0.975	0.99
v				
1	3.078	6.314	12.706	31.821
2	1.886	2.920	4.303	6.965
3	1.638	2.353	3.182	4.541
4	1.533	2.132	2.776	3.747
5	1.476	2.015	2.571	3.365
6	1.440	1.943	2.447	3.143
7	1.415	1.895	2.365	2.998
8	1.397	1.860	2.306	2.896
9	1.383	1.833	2.262	2.821
10	1.372	1.812	2.228	2.764

Confidence intervals

The *t*-distribution can be used to find a confidence interval for the population mean μ of a normally distributed population whose variance is unknown.

Suppose that a particular sample is taken and the recorded values are $x_1, x_2, \ldots, x_n$. The value of S^2 for this particular sample is s^2, where

$$s^2 = \frac{(x_1 - \bar{x})^2 + (x_2 - \bar{x})^2 + \ldots + (x_n - \bar{x})^2}{n-1} = \frac{\sum x_i^2 - n\bar{x}^2}{n-1}$$

The method of constructing a confidence interval for μ is similar to that used before, except that

• s replaces σ

• the *t*-distribution with $n-1$ degrees of freedom replaces the standard normal distribution

For example, suppose we want a 95% confidence interval from a random sample of size 10.

The number of degrees of freedom is $10 - 1 = 9$.

We need the percentage point for $p = 0.975$, as you can see from the diagram.

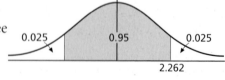

From the table above, the corresponding value is 2.262.

So the 95% confidence interval is from $\bar{x} - 2.262\left(\dfrac{s}{\sqrt{10}}\right)$ to $\bar{x} + 2.262\left(\dfrac{s}{\sqrt{10}}\right)$.

E1 The heights in metres of trees in a forest are normally distributed with unknown mean and variance. A random sample of 15 trees is selected. For this sample, $\bar{x} = 28.5$ and $s^2 = 18.2$.

(a) Write down the number of degrees of freedom for this situation.

(b) Find the appropriate percentage point for a 95% confidence interval.

(c) Construct a 95% confidence interval for the mean height of trees in the forest.

K A 95% confidence interval for the population mean μ of a normally distributed random variable, based on a sample of size n, is

$$\bar{x} - t_{n-1}\left(\frac{s}{\sqrt{n}}\right) \text{ to } \bar{x} + t_{n-1}\left(\frac{s}{\sqrt{n}}\right)$$

where $s^2 = \dfrac{\Sigma x_i^2 - n\bar{x}^2}{n-1}$ and t_{n-1} is the value from the percentage points table of the t-distribution with $n-1$ degrees of freedom for which $p = 0.975$ (so that 95% of the distribution is between $-t_{n-1}$ and t_{n-1}).

Other confidence intervals are found in a similar way. For example, for a 90% confidence interval the corresponding value of p is 0.95 (so that 90% of the distribution is between $-t_{n-1}$ and t_{n-1}).

Intervals may be written using brackets. For example, the interval from 290 to 310 may be written as (290, 310).

Example 6

The weights of the fish of a certain species in a lake are normally distributed with unknown mean and variance. A biologist takes a random sample of 10 fish. Their weights in grams are

342   378   368   380   371   378   367   368   347   354

(a) Find a 90% confidence interval for the mean weight of the fish in the lake.

(b) The biologist reads a report claiming that the mean weight of fish of this species is 380 g. What do her own results suggest about this value?

Solution

(a) $\bar{x} = \dfrac{342 + 378 + \ldots + 354}{10} = 365.3$

$\Sigma x_i^2 - n\bar{x}^2 = 342^2 + \ldots + 354^2 - 10 \times 365.3^2 = 1594.1$

So $s^2 = \dfrac{\Sigma x_i^2 - n\bar{x}^2}{n-1} = \dfrac{1594.1}{9} = 177.12$, from which $s = \sqrt{177.12} = 13.31$

$n = 10$, so the number of degrees of freedom $= 10 - 1 = 9$.

For a 90% confidence interval we need the percentage point for $p = 0.95$ (as shown in the diagram).

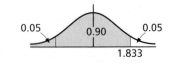

From the table, the corresponding value is 1.833.

So the confidence interval is from $\bar{x} - 1.833\left(\dfrac{s}{\sqrt{n}}\right)$ to $\bar{x} + 1.833\left(\dfrac{s}{\sqrt{n}}\right)$

that is, from $365.3 - 1.833 \times \dfrac{13.31}{\sqrt{10}}$ to $365.3 + 1.833 \times \dfrac{13.31}{\sqrt{10}}$, or (357.6, 373.0).

(b) The value 380 g is outside the 95% confidence interval. This suggests either that the claim in the report may be incorrect, or that the fish in this particular lake may be underweight.

Exercise E (answers p 127)

1 The times taken by a random sample of 8 ten-year-old children to solve a shape puzzle were (in seconds): 23, 34, 29, 28, 30, 36, 25, 35

  You may assume that the times taken by ten-year-olds to solve the puzzle have a normal distribution.

  (a) Find an unbiased estimate of the mean of this distribution.

  (b) Find an unbiased estimate of the variance of the distribution.

  (c) Construct a 95% confidence interval for the mean of the distribution.

2 The weights of the adult apes in a colony are believed to be normally distributed. Some zoologists capture a random sample of 20 apes from the colony and record the weight, x kg, of each ape. They find that

  $$\Sigma x = 1347.2 \text{ and } \Sigma x^2 = 91\,496.15$$

  (a) Find an unbiased estimate of

  (i) the mean weight of the adults in the colony

  (ii) the variance of the weights of the adults in the colony

  (b) Construct a 95% confidence interval for the mean weight of the adults in the colony.

  (c) A previous researcher claimed that the mean weight of the apes was 64.5 kg. Is this value consistent with the result obtained from the present sample?

3 A factory makes electrical components that are intended to have approximately the same resistance. A random sample of 12 components is selected and the resistance, in ohms, of each component is measured. The results are:

  14.3   15.1   14.0   14.7   14.2   15.0   14.1   13.9   14.7   14.6   15.2   14.3

  (a) Construct a 90% confidence interval for the mean resistance of the components made by the factory.

  (b) State the assumption you need to make in order to carry out the calculation in (a).

4 The flight times, x minutes, from airport A to airport B were recorded on 14 occasions during a particular week and it was found that

  $$\Sigma x = 1337 \text{ and } \Sigma x^2 = 128\,050$$

  The flight times may be assumed to be a random sample from a normal distribution.

  (a) Calculate unbiased estimates of the mean, μ, and the variance, σ^2, of the flight times.

  (b) Calculate a 95% confidence interval for μ.   AQA 2003

Key points

- $\bar{x}$ is an unbiased estimate of the population mean μ. (p 64)

- $s^2 = \dfrac{\sum x_i^2 - n\bar{x}^2}{n-1}$ is an unbiased estimate of the population variance σ^2. (p 65)

- A confidence interval for the population mean μ of a normally distributed random variable, based on a sample of size n, takes the form

$$\bar{x} - t_{n-1}\left(\frac{s}{\sqrt{n}}\right) \text{ to } \bar{x} + t_{n-1}\left(\frac{s}{\sqrt{n}}\right)$$

  where t_{n-1} is the appropriate percentage point of the t-distribution with $n-1$ degrees of freedom. (p 72)

Test yourself (answers p 127)

1 As part of a quality control procedure, the manager of a bottling plant regularly takes random samples of 20 bottles from the production line and measures the contents, $x$cl, of each bottle. On one occasion, he finds that

$$\sum x = 1518.9 \quad \text{and} \quad \sum x^2 = 115\,360.15$$

Assuming that the contents are normally distributed, find a 95% confidence interval for the mean. AQA 2002

2 Charles is an athlete specialising in throwing the javelin. During practice, he throws the following distances, in metres.

40.3   39.8   41.6   42.8   39.0   38.6   40.8   41.1

(a) Calculate unbiased estimates of the mean and the variance of the distance thrown.

(b) (i) Hence calculate a 95% confidence interval for the mean distance thrown.

   (ii) State two assumptions that you need to make in order to do this calculation. AQA 2003

3 A medical statistician is studying the weights, $x$kg, of newborn babies in a hospital. She finds that, in a certain month, 25 babies were born in this hospital and that for these babies $\sum x = 88.2$ and $\sum x^2 = 326.2$.

(a) (i) Calculate unbiased estimates of the mean and variance of the weights of babies born in this hospital.

   (ii) Assuming that the weights are normally distributed, calculate a 99% confidence interval for the mean weight of babies born in this hospital.

(b) She subsequently reads in a report that the mean weight of babies born in her region is 4.1 kg. Comment on her results with reference to this report. AQA 2002

Proof that $E(S^2) = \sigma^2$

In order to show this, we have to assume two general results that we have not yet proved:

The expectation of the sum of random variables is the sum of their expectations:

$$E(X + Y + Z + ...) = E(X) + E(Y) + E(Z) + ... \tag{1}$$

The variance of the sum of **independent** random variables is the sum of their variances:

$$\text{If } X, Y, ... \text{ are independent, } \text{Var}(X + Y + ...) = \text{Var}(X) + \text{Var}(Y) + ... \tag{2}$$

We have already shown, in chapter 1, that $\text{Var}(aX) = a^2\text{Var}(X)$. $\hspace{2cm}$ (3)

We also need the result, again shown in chapter 1, that $\hspace{1cm} \text{Var}(X) = E(X^2) - [E(X)]^2$

$$\text{from which} \hspace{1cm} E(X^2) = [E(X)]^2 + \text{Var}(X) \tag{4}$$

Let $X_1, X_2, ..., X_n$ be n independent random variables, each with the same mean μ and the same variance σ^2.

First we need to prove that $E(\overline{X}) = \mu$ and that $\text{Var}(\overline{X}) = \dfrac{\sigma^2}{n}$.

$$E(\overline{X}) = E\left(\frac{X_1 + X_2 + ... + X_n}{n}\right) = \frac{E(X_1) + E(X_2) + ... + E(X_n)}{n} = \frac{n\mu}{n} = \mu \hspace{1cm} \text{from (1)}$$

$$\text{Var}(\overline{X}) = \text{Var}\left(\frac{X_1 + ... + X_n}{n}\right) = \frac{1}{n^2}[\text{Var}(X_1) + ... + \text{Var}(X_n)] = \frac{1}{n^2}\left(n\sigma^2\right) = \frac{\sigma^2}{n} \hspace{0.5cm} \text{from (2), (3)}$$

Then we need to prove a familiar result:
$$\begin{aligned}
\sum(X_i - \overline{X})^2 &= \sum(X_i^2 - 2\overline{X}X_i + \overline{X}^2) \\
&= \sum X_i^2 - 2\overline{X}\sum X_i + n\overline{X}^2 \\
&= \sum X_i^2 - 2\overline{X}(n\overline{X}) + n\overline{X}^2 \\
&= \sum X_i^2 - n\overline{X}^2
\end{aligned}$$

Now take expected values, and use (1): $\hspace{1cm} E[\sum(X_i - \overline{X})^2] = \sum E(X_i^2) - nE(\overline{X}^2) \tag{5}$

By using (4) above, first for X_i and then for $\overline{X}$, we get:
$$\begin{aligned}
E(X_i^2) &= [E(X_i)]^2 + \text{Var}(X_i) \\
&= \mu^2 + \sigma^2 \\
E(\overline{X}^2) &= [E(\overline{X})]^2 + \text{Var}(\overline{X}) \\
&= \mu^2 + \frac{\sigma^2}{n}
\end{aligned}$$

Substituting these expressions into (5), we get:
$$\begin{aligned}
E[\sum(X_i - \overline{X})^2] &= n(\mu^2 + \sigma^2) - n\left(\mu^2 + \frac{\sigma^2}{n}\right) \\
&= (n-1)\sigma^2
\end{aligned}$$

It follows that $\hspace{0.3cm} E\left[\dfrac{\sum(X_i - \overline{X})^2}{n-1}\right] = \sigma^2.$

5 Hypothesis testing

In this chapter you will learn

- what is meant by null hypothesis, alternative hypothesis, significance level, test statistic, critical value, critical region, Type I and Type II errors, one-tailed and two-tailed tests
- how to test for the mean of a normal distribution with either known or unknown variance
- how to test for the mean of a distribution using a normal approximation

A Basic ideas of hypothesis testing (answers p 128)

A person claims to have the ability to predict the outcome of a throw of a coin.

In order to test this claim, the person is asked to predict the outcomes of four throws. All four of his predictions turn out to be correct.

A1 If the person has no special ability but is just guessing, then the probability that each individual prediction is correct is $\frac{1}{2}$.

    (a) What is the probability that all four predictions will be correct?

    (b) Do you think that there is sufficient evidence that the person has some ability to predict the outcome of a throw?

Four is a small number of trials. A new test is to be carried out in which the person will be asked to predict the outcomes of 20 throws.

If the person is just guessing, then as before the probability of predicting an outcome correctly is $\frac{1}{2}$. So we would expect about 10 predictions to be correct. If he gets a lot more than 10 correct, then that would be evidence of some ability to predict.

The number of correct predictions out of 20 follows the binomial distribution with $n = 20$ and $p = \frac{1}{2}$.

Part of the table of cumulative probabilities for this distribution is shown on the right.

From the table we can find the probability of getting, for example, 12 or more predictions correct, like this:

P(12 or more correct) = 1 − P(up to 11 correct)

$$= 1 - 0.7483 = 0.2517$$

Before the test is carried out, we have to decide how many predictions will need to be correct for us to be convinced that the result is not due to just guessing.

x	Probability that number of correct predictions $\leq x$
10	0.5881
11	0.7483
12	0.8684
13	0.9432
14	0.9793
15	0.9941
16	0.9987
17	0.9998
18	1.0000
19	1.0000
20	1.0000

A2 Would you be convinced if the number of correct predictions were

    (a) 12 or more   (b) 13 or more   (c) 14 or more   (d) 15 or more

A **hypothesis** is a statement which may be true or may be false – we do not yet know.

In the example discussed so far, there are two hypotheses we have to decide between:

(1) The person has no special ability but is just guessing.

(2) The person has some ability to predict.

In terms of probability, these two hypotheses can be restated as:

(1) The probability of correctly predicting the outcome of a throw is $\frac{1}{2}$.

(2) The probability of correctly predicting the outcome of a throw is greater than $\frac{1}{2}$.

Unless the evidence is very convincing, then it is the first hypothesis that we will accept. This hypothesis is the **null hypothesis**. It says that this person is no different from anyone else.

The other hypothesis is the **alternative hypothesis**.

If the null hypothesis is true, then from the table on the opposite page the probability of correctly predicting 15 or more outcomes out of 20 is $1 - 0.9793 = 0.0207$, or approximately 2%.

We may decide that getting a result with a probability of only 2% is enough to make us reject the null hypothesis. If so, then 2% is called the **level of significance** of the result of the test.

If we decide to set the level of significance at 2%, then we will accept the null hypothesis if the person correctly predicts 14 outcomes or fewer, but reject it if the person correctly predicts 15 or more.

A3 The person is asked to predict the outcomes of 30 throws. Cumulative probabilities based on the null hypothesis are shown in the table on the right.

(a) The tester decides to reject the null hypothesis if the number of correct predictions is 19 or more. What level of significance (to the nearest 1%) is the tester using?

(b) If the level of significance is set at 5%, what is the smallest number of correct predictions that would lead to rejection of the null hypothesis?

The level of significance of a test shows how convincing the evidence is: the smaller the level of significance, the more convincing is the evidence.

x	Probability that number of correct predictions $\leq x$
15	0.5722
16	0.7077
17	0.8192
18	0.8998
19	0.9506
20	0.9786
21	0.9919
22	0.9974
23	0.9993
24	0.9998
25	1.0000
26	1.0000
27	1.0000
28	1.0000
29	1.0000
30	1.0000

B Mean of a normal distribution with known variance (answers p 128)

The next example of hypothesis testing introduces some other commonly used terms.

Imagine that a car engine is modified to try to increase the maximum speed of the car.

The maximum speed in m.p.h. of cars with unmodified engines is known to be distributed normally with mean 125 and standard deviation 3.5.

It will be assumed that the modification may affect the mean but will not affect the variance. So the standard deviation is unchanged.

The null hypothesis, denoted by H_0, is that the mean maximum speed μ of the modified cars has not increased, so μ is still 125.

The alternative hypothesis H_1 is that the mean maximum speed has increased, so that $\mu > 125$.

H_0: $\mu = 125$

H_1: $\mu > 125$

Test statistic

In order to test the effect of the modification, a random sample of 10 modified cars is to be selected and the cars' maximum speeds measured.

We know that the sample mean $\overline{X}$ is a random variable that is normally distributed with mean μ, variance $\dfrac{\sigma^2}{n}$ and standard deviation, or standard error, $\left(\dfrac{\sigma}{\sqrt{n}}\right)$.

We shall use the value of $\overline{X}$ to decide between the two hypotheses.
$\overline{X}$ is the **test statistic**.

Critical value, critical region, acceptance region

If hypothesis H_0 is true, then $\mu = 125$ and $\sigma = 3.5$.

So $\overline{X}$ will be normally distributed with mean 125 and standard error $\dfrac{3.5}{\sqrt{10}} = 1.11$ (to 2 d.p.).

The diagram shows the distribution of $\overline{X}$ in relation to the standard normal distribution.

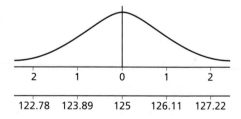

We will reject H_0 if the value of $\overline{X}$ that we get is so large that it would be very unlikely to happen if H_0 is true.

'Very unlikely' is usually taken to mean 'with probability 5%'.
5% is the level of significance of the test that we shall use.

Let Z be the standardised variable corresponding to $\overline{X}$. So $Z = \dfrac{\overline{X} - \mu}{\left(\dfrac{\sigma}{\sqrt{n}}\right)} = \dfrac{\overline{X} - 125}{\left(\dfrac{3.5}{\sqrt{10}}\right)}$.

Z has the standard normal distribution.

The percentage points table of the standard normal distribution tells us that there is a 0.05, or 5%, probability that Z will be greater than 1.6449.

So if the value of Z turns out to be greater than 1.6449, we will reject H_0.

1.6449 is called the **critical value** of Z.

The region $Z > 1.6449$, which contains all the values of Z for which H_0 will be rejected, is called the **critical region** of the test.

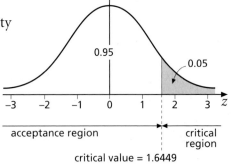

critical value = 1.6449

The region $Z < 1.6449$, which contains all the values of Z for which H_0 will be accepted, is called the **acceptance region**. Both regions are shown in the diagram.

The critical value and critical region of a hypothesis test are worked out before the actual sample values are considered.

z-statistic

Suppose that a random sample of 10 modified cars gives the following set of maximum speeds:

   123   128   132   125   123   128   131   130   123   126

We use lower-case letters for values obtained from a particular sample.

The value of $\overline{X}$ for this sample is denoted by $\bar{x}$.

$$\bar{x} = \frac{123 + 128 + \ldots + 126}{10} = 126.9$$

The value of Z for this sample is denoted by z, where $z = \dfrac{\bar{x} - \mu}{\left(\dfrac{\sigma}{\sqrt{n}}\right)}$.

So $z = \dfrac{126.9 - 125}{\left(\dfrac{3.5}{\sqrt{10}}\right)} = 1.7167$.

We now compare the value of z with the critical value, which is 1.6449.

$z > 1.6449$, so the value of z is in the critical region. So we reject H_0 and accept H_1.

So there is evidence, at the 5% level, that the the mean maximum speed has increased.

Note

The critical region may also be expressed in terms of the non-standardised $\overline{X}$.

$Z > 1.6449$ becomes $\overline{X} > \mu + 1.6449 \left(\dfrac{\sigma}{\sqrt{n}}\right)$,

that is $\overline{X} > 125 + 1.6449 \left(\dfrac{3.5}{\sqrt{10}}\right)$, or $\overline{X} > 126.82$.

The process of carrying out a hypothesis test is summarised below.
The car engines test is used as an example.

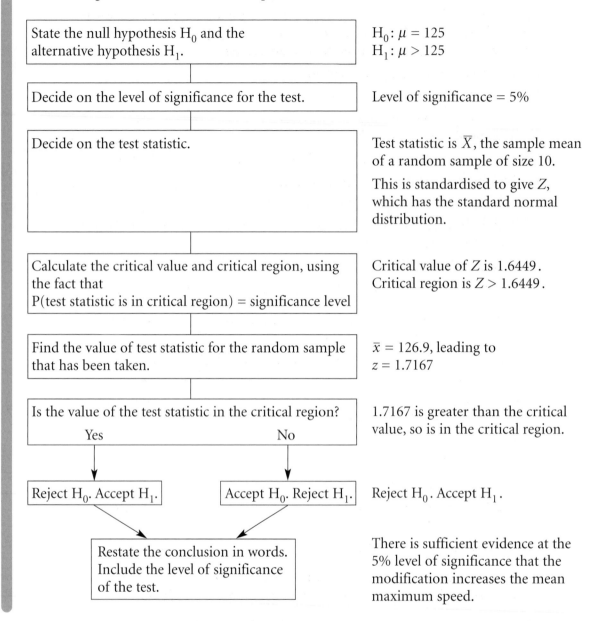

| State the null hypothesis H_0 and the alternative hypothesis H_1. | $H_0: \mu = 125$
 $H_1: \mu > 125$ |

| Decide on the level of significance for the test. | Level of significance = 5% |

| Decide on the test statistic. | Test statistic is $\bar{X}$, the sample mean of a random sample of size 10.

 This is standardised to give Z, which has the standard normal distribution. |

| Calculate the critical value and critical region, using the fact that
 P(test statistic is in critical region) = significance level | Critical value of Z is 1.6449.
 Critical region is $Z > 1.6449$. |

| Find the value of test statistic for the random sample that has been taken. | $\bar{x} = 126.9$, leading to
 $z = 1.7167$ |

| Is the value of the test statistic in the critical region?
 Yes   No | 1.7167 is greater than the critical value, so is in the critical region. |

Reject H_0. Accept H_1.   Accept H_0. Reject H_1.   Reject H_0. Accept H_1.

Restate the conclusion in words. Include the level of significance of the test.

There is sufficient evidence at the 5% level of significance that the modification increases the mean maximum speed.

The 5% level of significance is the one most often used in practice. Using it is equivalent to saying that if something happens whose probability, according to the null hypothesis, is only 5%, then that counts as convincing evidence against the hypothesis. Of course, the null hypothesis may still be true, in which case the probability of rejecting it wrongly is 5%.

If the consequences of making a wrong decision are very serious, then the level of significance may be made more stringent, say 1%. In this case the evidence needed to reject the null hypothesis has to be more convincing. A more extreme value of the test statistic would be required.

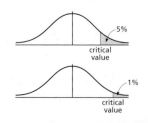

B1 The weights of tomatoes grown in a market garden are normally distributed with mean 55.2 g and standard deviation 3.8 g.

A new kind of plant treatment is claimed to increase the weights of the tomatoes. In order to test this claim, some of the plants are treated and then a random sample of 50 of the tomatoes from these plants is selected.

The mean weight of the sample is 56.3 g.

Assume that the standard deviation of the weights is unchanged.

(a) The null hypothesis for the test is $H_0: \mu = 55.2$.
State the alternative hypothesis.

If H_0 is true, then the sample mean $\overline{X}$ is normally distributed with mean 55.2.

(b) Find the standard deviation (standard error) of $\overline{X}$.

The level of significance for the test is to be 5%.

(c) Find the appropriate percentage point of the standard normal distribution. This is the critical value of Z.

(d) Find the value of z for the sample.

(e) Compare the value of z with the critical value and state the test conclusion.

B2 A factory produces batteries whose lifetimes are normally distributed with mean 94 hours and standard deviation 3.3 hours.

A modification to the manufacturing process is carried out which is intended to increase the mean lifetime. It has no effect on the standard deviation.

In order to test whether the modification has been effective, a random sample of 20 batteries is selected. The mean lifetime of this sample is 95.5 hours.

The level of significance is to be **1%**.

(a) State the null and alternative hypotheses.

(b) Find the standard error of $\overline{X}$.

(c) Find the appropriate percentage point of the standard normal distribution for the 1% level of significance.

(d) Carry out the test using the z-statistic and state your conclusion.

B3 Redo question B2 but at the 5% level of significance. Do you come to a different conclusion? If so, explain why the conclusions are different.

B4 A firm makes elastic bands. The maximum length to which a band can be stretched before breaking is normally distributed with mean 235 mm and standard deviation 48 mm. A researcher claims that the mean maximum length is increased when a different material is used. It is planned to test this claim at the 5% level of significance by taking a random sample of 15 bands and using $\overline{X}$ as the test statistic.

(a) Write down the critical region of this test in the form $Z > \ldots$, where Z is the standardised variable corresponding to $\overline{X}$.

(b) Find the standard error of $\overline{X}$ and hence express the critical region in the form $\overline{X} > \ldots$

One-tailed and two-tailed tests

In the previous examples, the purpose of the modification or treatment was to increase the maximum speed, weight or lifetime. So the purpose of the test was to see if there was evidence that μ had increased.

Suppose instead that car engines are modified in a way that might lead to a higher or a lower maximum speed. So the purpose of the test is to see whether μ has changed – either increased or decreased.

If the null hypothesis is $H_0: \mu = 125$, then the alternative hypothesis is $H_1: \mu \neq 125$.

In this case either very low or very high values of the test statistic will indicate that μ has changed as a result of the modification.

There are two critical values, an upper value and a lower value.

The critical region consists of two parts, a high value part and a low value part.

The acceptance region lies between the two critical values.

If the level of significance is to be 5%, the probability of 0.05 is split equally between the two parts, as shown here.

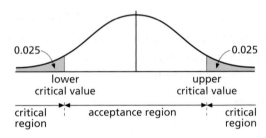

The test in this case is called a **two-tailed test**. (The 'tails' are the parts of the distribution beyond each critical value.)

The test used in the previous examples is a **one-tailed test**.

> Use a one-tailed test when H_1 is of the form $\mu > \ldots$ or of the form $\mu < \ldots$
>
> Use a two-tailed test when H_1 is of the form $\mu \neq \ldots$

B5 Ten years ago it was found that the weights in grams of animals of a certain species were normally distributed with mean 84.0 and standard deviation 3.2.

Since that time climatic conditions have changed and this may have affected the mean weight. It is assumed that the standard deviation has not changed.

In order to test whether the mean weight has changed, a random sample of 20 animals will be selected and the mean weight of the sample will be used as test statistic. The level of significance will be 5%.

(a) The null hypothesis is $H_0: \mu = 84.0$. What is the alternative hypothesis?

(b) Let $\overline{X}$ be the mean weight of a random sample of 20 animals. If the null hypothesis is true, $\overline{X}$ is normally distributed with mean 84.0. What is its standard error?

(c) If Z is the standardised variable corresponding to $\overline{X}$, then the upper critical value of Z is such that 2.5% of the distribution is above it.
Use the percentage points table to find the upper critical value.

(d) Find the lower critical value and state the acceptance region.

(e) When the random sample is taken, the sample mean $\overline{x}$ is 82.4.
Find the value of z for this sample.

(f) What conclusion do you draw?

K To test a hypothesis about the mean of a normal distribution with known variance, the standard normal distribution is used to find the critical region.

If the value of z for the sample, where $z = \dfrac{\bar{x} - \mu}{\left(\dfrac{\sigma}{\sqrt{n}}\right)}$, is in the critical region, H_0 is rejected.

Example 1

The amount of liquid that a filling machine pours into a bottle is normally distributed with mean 155 ml and standard deviation 2.5 ml.

After a breakdown and repair of the machine, it is suspected that the mean amount put into a bottle may have changed.

A random sample of 50 bottles yields a mean amount of 154.2 ml per bottle.

Assuming that the standard deviation of the amount is unchanged, investigate at the 1% level of significance the claim that the mean amount put into a bottle by the machine has not changed.

Solution

Let μ be the mean amount in ml after the breakdown and repair.

The two hypotheses are

$H_0: \mu = 155$

$H_1: \mu \neq 155$

Let $\bar{X}$ be the mean amount for a sample of size 50.

If H_0 is true, then $\bar{X}$ is normally distributed with mean 155 and standard deviation $\dfrac{2.5}{\sqrt{50}} = 0.3536$ (to 4 d.p.).

So Z, which is $\dfrac{\bar{X} - 155}{0.3536}$, has the standard normal distribution.

Because the mean amount may have increased or decreased, a two-tailed test is needed.

Each tail will contain 0.5% of the distribution, or probability 0.005.

The diagram on the right shows that we need the percentage point with 0.995 below it.

From the percentage points table, this is 2.5758.

So the upper critical value is 2.5758 and the lower critical value is −2.5758.

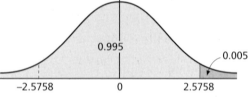

For the sample, $z = \dfrac{\bar{x} - 155}{0.3536} = \dfrac{154.2 - 155}{0.3536} = -2.262$ (to 3 d.p.)

This is not in the critical region.
So there is insufficient evidence, at the 1% level, to reject H_0.

Conclusion: Accept, at the 1% level of significance, that the mean amount poured by the machine has not changed.

Exercise B (answers p 128)

1 The heights in cm of five-year-old pine trees are normally distributed with mean 125.6 and standard deviation 12.2. A supplier claims to sell seedlings that grow to be taller than average. A gardener buys 12 seedlings from the supplier and grows them for five years. Their heights are then

> 131 145 128 118 136 152 163 124 171 145 138 137

Test the supplier's claim at the 5% significance level.

2 A machine is set up to make bolts whose diameter is normally distributed with mean 5 mm and standard deviation 0.4 mm. After repairs to the machine, a random sample of 10 bolts is taken and these are found to have a mean diameter of 5.28 mm.

Test at the 5% significance level whether the mean diameter of the bolts made by the machine has changed.

3 A rope manufacturer claims that its ropes have a breaking strain that is normally distributed with mean 50 newtons and standard deviation 1.2 newtons. A random sample of rope sections is taken and the breaking strain of each is measured, with the following results:

> 52.0 50.5 49.4 49.3 49.7 48.7 52.8 51.1 51.3 50.7 51.2

Test at the 2% level of significance the manufacturer's claim that the mean breaking strain of the rope is 50 newtons. Assume that the standard deviation is 1.2.

4 The wavelength in microns of a radioactive source A is known to be normally distributed with mean 1.622 and standard deviation 0.004. Nine random measurements of an unidentified radioactive sample are taken and give wavelengths of

> 1.612 1.622 1.613 1.621 1.609 1.618 1.624 1.625 1.622

Test at the 10% significance level whether this sample could be from source A.

5 The lightbulbs produced by a company have lifetimes that are normally distributed with mean 1250 hours and standard deviation 62 hours. A modification to the manufacturing process is claimed to increase the mean lifetime. To test this claim the lifetimes of a random sample of 15 of the modified bulbs are measured. The mean lifetime of the sample is 1274 hours. Investigate the claim.

6 A random variable X is normally distributed with mean μ and standard deviation 3.6. The null hypothesis $H_0 : \mu = 30$ is to be tested against the alternative hypothesis $H_1 : \mu \neq 30$ using the 5% level of significance.

The mean $\overline{X}$ of a random sample of 20 observations is to be used as the test statistic.

(a) Write down the distribution of $\overline{X}$ assuming H_0 is true.

(b) Find the acceptance region for $\overline{X}$, giving its limits to two decimal places.

(c) When the sample is taken, the mean value of the sample is found to be 36.2. What conclusion do you draw?

C Mean of a normal distribution with unknown variance

(answers p 129)

Suppose that the weight of potatoes grown in ordinary soil is normally distributed with mean 48 g but with unknown variance.

A horticulturalist develops a new kind of soil and claims that it increases the mean weight of potatoes grown in it.

Let μ be the mean weight in grams of potatoes grown in the new soil.

The null hypothesis is that $\mu = 48$ and the alternative hypothesis is that $\mu > 48$. So a one-tailed test is appropriate.

The test will be based on a random sample of 20 potatoes grown in the new soil.

However, we cannot use the test statistic $\overline{X}$ or Z in the same way as before, because we do not know the variance.

We have met this situation when finding confidence intervals. We use the sample itself to give an estimate of the population variance.

The random variable $S^2 = \dfrac{\sum X_i^2 - n\overline{X}^2}{n-1}$ is an unbiased estimator of σ^2.

The formula for Z, which we use when the variance is known, is $Z = \dfrac{\overline{X} - \mu}{\left(\dfrac{\sigma}{\sqrt{n}}\right)}$.

If we replace σ by S, we get $\dfrac{\overline{X} - \mu}{\left(\dfrac{S}{\sqrt{n}}\right)}$, which has the t-distribution with

$(n-1)$ degrees of freedom.

We use the t-distribution instead of the normal distribution to find the critical value and the critical region.

If the level of significance is to be 5%, we need the corresponding percentage point of the t-distribution with 19 degrees of freedom.

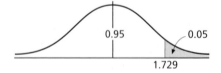

From the table of percentage points, this is 1.729.

So the critical value is 1.729.

From the random sample we need to find both $\bar{x}$ and s^2.

s^2 is the particular value of S^2 for the sample, and is given by $s^2 = \dfrac{\sum x_i^2 - n\bar{x}^2}{n-1}$.

Instead of the z-statistic $\dfrac{\bar{x} - \mu}{\left(\dfrac{\sigma}{\sqrt{n}}\right)}$ we use the **t-statistic** $t = \dfrac{\bar{x} - \mu}{\left(\dfrac{s}{\sqrt{n}}\right)}$.

Suppose a random sample of size 20 gives $\bar{x} = 48.92$ and $s^2 = 5.12$.

For this sample, $t = \dfrac{\bar{x} - \mu}{\left(\dfrac{s}{\sqrt{n}}\right)} = \dfrac{48.92 - 48}{\left(\dfrac{\sqrt{5.12}}{\sqrt{20}}\right)} = 1.8183$. This is greater than 1.729, so reject H_0.

C1 A machine puts vegetables into sacks that are meant to have a mean weight of 10 kg.

The supervisor suspects that the machine is not working properly and that the mean weight μ kg of the sacks has increased.

It may be assumed that the weights are normally distributed.

(a) State the null hypothesis and the alternative hypothesis.

(b) Is the appropriate test a one-tailed test or a two-tailed test?

The supervisor weighs a random sample of 20 sacks. Their weights are

| 10.5 | 10.8 | 9.8 | 9.7 | 10.5 | 9.9 | 9.8 | 10.1 | 9.9 | 10.1 |
| 9.8 | 9.8 | 10.8 | 10.0 | 10.3 | 9.8 | 10.2 | 10.1 | 10.2 | 9.7 |

(c) The supervisor wishes to test at the 5% level. Use the percentage points table for the t-distribution to find the critical value(s).

(d) Find the value of $\bar{x}$ for this sample.

(e) Find the value of s^2 for this sample.

(f) Find the value of t for this sample.

(g) State the conclusion of the test.

C2 A student reads that the mean weight of babies born in her local hospital ten years ago was 3.45 kg. She decides to investigate whether there has been any change in the mean weight since then.

She collects records of births and draws from them a random sample of 25 birth weights. For this sample, $\Sigma x_i = 88$ and $\Sigma x_i^2 = 310.4$.

(a) State the null and alternative hypotheses.

(b) Is the appropriate test a one-tailed test or a two-tailed test?

Assume that babies' birth weights are normally distributed and that the level of significance is 5%.

(c) Find the critical value(s) using the t-distribution.

(d) For the student's sample find

    (i) the value of $\bar{x}$

    (ii) the value of s^2

    (iii) the value of t

(e) State the conclusion of the test.

K To test a hypothesis about the mean of a normal distribution with unknown variance, the t-distribution is used to find the critical region.

The variance is estimated from the sample using the formula $s^2 = \dfrac{\Sigma x_i^2 - n\bar{x}^2}{n-1}$.

If the value of t for the sample, where $t = \dfrac{\bar{x} - \mu}{\left(\dfrac{s}{\sqrt{n}}\right)}$, is in the critical region, H_0 is rejected.

Example 2

15 snakes of a certain species were selected at random and their lengths measured. The lengths in cm were as follows.

135 141 132 138 136 129 142 130 131 133 136 138 135 134 135

Investigate, at the 5% level of significance, the claim that these snakes are drawn from a normally distributed population with mean 133 cm.

You are given that $\Sigma x_i = 2025$, $\Sigma x_i^2 = 273\,571$.

Solution

The null hypothesis is $H_0 : \mu = 133$

The alternative hypothesis is $H_1 : \mu \neq 133$

Because the null hypothesis would be rejected if the sample mean were either very high or very low, a two-tailed test is needed.

The variance of the population is unknown, so the t-distribution will be used to find the critical values and critical region.

To find the critical values we need the 97.5 percentage point of the t-distribution with $15 - 1 = 14$ degrees of freedom.

From the tables, this is 2.145.

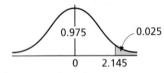

So the upper critical value is 2.145 and the lower -2.145.

The next step is to calculate the t-statistic $\dfrac{\bar{x} - \mu}{\left(\frac{s}{\sqrt{n}}\right)}$ for the given sample.

$$\bar{x} = \frac{2025}{15} = 135 \qquad s^2 = \frac{\Sigma x_i^2 - n\bar{x}^2}{n-1} = \frac{273\,571 - 15 \times 135^2}{15 - 1} = \frac{196}{14} = 14$$

So $t = \dfrac{135 - 133}{\left(\frac{\sqrt{14}}{\sqrt{15}}\right)} = 2.0702$

s may also be found by entering the data 135, 141, ... into a calculator and using the s_{n-1} key.

This value is not in the critical region, so H_0 is accepted.

Conclusion: At the 5% level of significance, the evidence shows that the sample could have been drawn from a population whose mean is 133 cm.

Exercise C (answers p 129)

1 Suppose the test in example 2 above is to be at the 10% level of significance.

   (a) Find the new upper and lower critical values and state the acceptance region of the test.

   (b) State the conclusion of the test.

2 The weight in kilograms of a certain breed of dog is normally distributed with mean 16.2. A breeder claims that he has developed this breed to produce dogs that are on average heavier.

To test this claim the editor of a dog fanciers' magazine arranges for a random sample of ten of the breeder's dogs to be weighed. The level of significance is to be 5%.

(a) State the null and alternative hypotheses for the mean weight μ.

(b) Is a one-tailed test or a two-tailed test needed in this case?

(c) Use the t-distribution with the appropriate number of degrees of freedom to find the critical value(s) and state the critical region.

The weights of the dogs in the sample are

    15.9   16.8   17.5   18.3   19.2   17.5   15.8   18.9   20.6   21.5

(d) Find the values of $\bar{x}$ and s^2 for this sample and hence calculate the value of the t-statistic.

(e) State the conclusion of the test.

3 Measurements of a water supply over a long period have shown that the mean concentration of a chemical, measured in parts per million, is 16.8. The concentration can be assumed to be normally distributed.

After a storm it is decided to test the water to see whether the mean concentration μ of the chemical has changed. Twenty samples of the water are taken at random and the concentration x measured. For this sample, $\Sigma x = 307.0$ and $\Sigma x^2 = 4811.25$.

(a) State appropriate null and alternative hypotheses for μ.

(b) Determine, at the 1% level of significance, whether there is evidence that the mean concentration of the chemical changed after the storm.

4 The 'lifetime' of a car tyre is measured by the number of miles it travels before needing replacement. The mean lifetime of tyres made by company A is 24 150 miles. Company B claims that its tyres are better and publishes the lifetimes of what it describes as 'ten typical tyres' made by the company:

    25 100 24 250 23 700 24 350 24 350 24 110 24 320 24 190 24 300 24 180

(a) State all the assumptions you need to make in order to carry out a hypothesis test using the data provided by company B.

(b) Making these assumptions, state the null and alternative hypotheses.

(c) Carry out the test at the 5% level of significance.

5 The weight of a certain species of rodent is known to be normally distributed with mean 0.675 kg. It is suspected that the rodents living on an island are heavier than average. The weights, w kg, of a random sample of 30 of the island rodents were measured. For this sample, $\Sigma w = 20.7$ and $\Sigma w^2 = 14.335$.

Test at the 5% level of significance whether the island rodents are heavier than average.

D Using a normal approximation

Up to now we have assumed that the random sample used in a hypothesis test has been drawn from a normally distributed population. This has justified using the z-statistic when the variance is known, and the t-statistic when the variance is unknown.

The central limit theorem states that if the sample size n is large enough, then the sample mean $\bar{X}$ is approximately normally distributed even if the sample is drawn from a non-normal population.

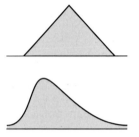

The size of sample needed to get a good approximation depends on the shape of the population distribution. If it is roughly similar to a normal distribution, with a peak at the centre, then even with fairly small samples the approximation will be good. If it is very asymmetric, larger samples are needed for a good approximation.

If nothing is known about the shape of the distribution, then the normal approximation can be used when $n \geq 30$.

As before, the z-statistic is used when the variance is known and the t-statistic when the variance is unknown.

> **K** If the distribution from which a random sample is taken is unknown, then provided the sample is sufficiently large ($n \geq 30$) the z-statistic (variance known) or the t-statistic (variance unknown) can be used to test a hypothesis about the population mean.

Example 3

An airport claims that the mean time for its security checks is 20 minutes. A researcher thinks it is longer than this and records the queuing times of 35 randomly selected passengers.

The mean $\bar{x}$ of the sample is 22.4 and the estimate s^2 of the population variance is 41.4.

Test at the 5% significance level whether the researcher's claim is justified.

Solution

The two hypotheses are $H_0: \mu = 20$
$\qquad\qquad\qquad\qquad\quad H_1: \mu > 20$

A one-sided test is appropriate.
The sample is large enough ($n = 35$) to assume that $\bar{X}$ is normally distributed.
The variance is unknown, so the t-distribution must be used, with $35 - 1 = 34$ d.f.

From tables, the percentage point for 95% below/5% above is 1.691. This is the critical value.

For the given sample, $t = \dfrac{22.4 - 20}{\left(\dfrac{\sqrt{41.4}}{\sqrt{35}}\right)} = 2.207$. This is greater than the critical value, so reject H_0.

So the researcher's claim is justified at the 5% level of significance.

Exercise D (answers p 130)

1 A brand of matches has on its boxes 'Average contents 48 matches'.
A student suspects that the mean number in a box is actually less than 48.
He buys 30 boxes from different sources and counts the number of
matches in each box. The results are

$$47 \quad 51 \quad 45 \quad 46 \quad 48 \quad 47 \quad 43 \quad 50 \quad 49 \quad 45 \quad 47 \quad 48 \quad 47 \quad 46 \quad 51$$

$$46 \quad 44 \quad 47 \quad 46 \quad 49 \quad 44 \quad 48 \quad 48 \quad 47 \quad 49 \quad 50 \quad 49 \quad 48 \quad 47 \quad 46$$

(a) Test at the 5% level of significance the student's suspicion.

(b) Explain why your method is appropriate, even though the distribution
of the number of matches in a box is unknown.

2 A local historian reads that the mean age at death of inhabitants of his area
ten years ago was 64.8 years. In order to find out whether this has changed,
he selects a random sample of 40 recent deaths and notes the age at death,
x years, for each one. For the sample, $\Sigma x = 2608$ and $\Sigma x^2 = 170\,120$.

(a) Test at the 5% level of significance whether the mean age of death has changed.

(b) Repeat the test, but at the 10% level of significance.

3 A student has a theory that the mean number of words in a sentence can be
used to help identify the writer of a story. She analyses the sentences in a
book by Alf Abita and finds that the mean sentence length is 14.8 words.

She has another book, written under a pen name, which she suspects is by
the same writer. She selects 35 sentences at random and counts the number, x,
of words in each sentence. She finds that $\Sigma x = 421$ and $\Sigma x^2 = 7206$.

Investigate at the 5% level of significance whether the mean number of
words per sentence in the second book could be 14.8.

4 The loaves made by a bread factory are labelled as weighing 0.8 kg.
However, to prevent accusations that loaves are underweight, the mean
weight of loaves made by the factory is actually 0.82 kg.

A consignment of these loaves is sent to a supermarket. As a quality control
exercise, 40 loaves are selected at random from the consignment and the weight,
x kg, of each loaf is recorded. It is found that $\Sigma x = 32.32$ and $\Sigma x^2 = 26.1787$.

Investigate at the 5% level of significance whether the mean weight of
the loaves in the consignment is different from 0.82 kg.

5 A food company claims that the mean meat content of its pies is 270 g and
the standard deviation 15 g. A laboratory analyses the meat content of a
random sample of 50 pies and finds that the mean meat content is 265.5 g.

(a) Assuming that the standard deviation is 15 g, test at the 2% level of significance
whether there is evidence that the mean meat content is different from what
the company states.

(b) Repeat the test, but at the 5% level of significance.

(c) How would you report the outcomes of the two tests in a way that
would make sense to a person who was not trained in statistics?

E Type I and Type II errors

Imagine that two species of animal, A and B, are very similar in appearance. The weights in grams of species A are normally distributed about a mean of 30 with a variance of 40. The weights of species B are normally distributed about a mean of 36 with a variance of 90.

A zoologist has found a colony of animals but does not know whether they are A or B. In her previous experience in the area, animals have all been of species A. So her null hypothesis is that the new colony is also A. Her two hypotheses are

$$H_0: \mu = 30, \sigma^2 = 40 \qquad H_1: \mu = 36, \sigma^2 = 90$$

The zoologist plans to take a sample of size 10; the significance level will be 5%.

If H_0 is true, then the sample mean, $\overline{X}$, of a sample of size 10 will be normally distributed with mean 30, variance $\frac{40}{10} = 4$ and standard error $\sqrt{4} = 2$.

The standardised variable corresponding to $\overline{X}$ is $Z = \dfrac{\overline{X} - 30}{2}$.

The critical value of Z for the 5% level of significance is 1.6449.

The corresponding value of $\overline{X}$ is $30 + 1.6449 \times 2 = 33.29$ (to 2 d.p.).

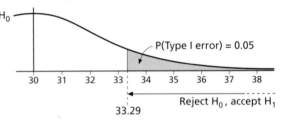

The diagram shows the distribution of $\overline{X}$ if H_0 is true.

If her sample mean $\bar{x}$ is greater than 33.29, the zoologist will reject H_0, because a value as large as this is unlikely to happen if H_0 is true.

But 'unlikely' does not mean impossible, and the zoologist might reject H_0 when it is true. This error – rejecting H_0 when it is true – is called a **Type I error**.

The probability of making this error if H_0 is true is 0.05. This is called the **size** of the Type I error. It is equal to the significance level.

If, however, H_1 is true, then $\overline{X}$ will be normally distributed with mean 36, variance $\frac{90}{10} = 9$ and standard error 3.

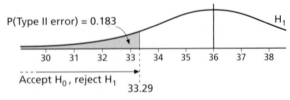

This diagram shows the distribution of $\overline{X}$ if H_1 is true.

If the value of $\bar{x}$ from her sample is less than 33.29, the zoologist will accept H_0 and reject H_1. But H_1 might still be true. Rejecting H_1 when it is true is a **Type II error**.

The size of this error is shown by the shading. It can be found from tables to be 0.183. (The size can be found only when H_1 specifies a value for μ.)

K A Type I error is to reject H_0 when it is true. Its size is equal to the significance level.

A Type II error is to reject H_1 when it is true.

Key points

- In a hypothesis test, the null hypothesis is denoted by H_0 and the alternative hypothesis by H_1. (p 78)

- The critical region is the set of values of the test statistic for which H_0 will be rejected. The acceptance region is the set for which H_0 will be accepted.
  If the level of significance is, say, 5% then the critical region is chosen so that the probability that the test statistic falls within it if H_0 is true is 0.05. (pp 78–80)

- Use a one-tailed test when H_1 is of the form $\mu > \ldots$ or of the form $\mu < \ldots$
  Use a two-tailed test when H_1 is of the form $\mu \neq \ldots$ (p 82)

- To test a hypothesis about the mean of a normal distribution with known variance, the standard normal distribution is used to find the critical region.
  If the value of z for the sample, where $z = \dfrac{\bar{x} - \mu}{\left(\dfrac{\sigma}{\sqrt{n}}\right)}$, is in the critical region, H_0 is rejected. (p 83)

- To test a hypothesis about the mean of a normal distribution with unknown variance, the t-distribution is used to find the critical region.
  If the value of t for the sample, where $t = \dfrac{\bar{x} - \mu}{\left(\dfrac{s}{\sqrt{n}}\right)}$, is in the critical region, H_0 is rejected. (p 86)

- If the distribution from which a random sample is taken is unknown, then if $n \geq 30$ the z-statistic (population variance known) or the t-statistic (population variance unknown) can be used to test a hypothesis about the population mean. (p 89)

- A Type I error is to reject H_0 when it is true. Its size is equal to the significance level.
  A Type II error is to reject H_1 when it is true. (p 91)

Mixed questions (answers p 130)

1 The fuel economy of a car is measured in litres per 100 km, so a lower figure indicates better fuel economy.

It is known that the fuel economy of cars of a certain model is normally distributed with mean 10.7 and **variance** 3.24. A garage owner modifies the engine and claims that modified cars have better fuel economy.
A consumers' organisation measures the fuel economy of a random sample of 15 modified cars and records the mean economy of the sample as 9.9.

Investigate, at the 5% significance level, the claim that the modification improves the mean fuel economy.

2 A casualty department claims that waiting times have fallen. The mean waiting time used to be 54.5 minutes. For a random sample of 35 waiting times, x minutes, it is found that $\sum x = 1820$ and $\sum x^2 = 96\,130$. Test the department's claim at the 1% level of significance.

3 Scores on IQ tests are designed to be normally distributed with mean 100 and standard deviation 15. A polling organisation uses a method of selecting people that is claimed to be random. However, a researcher suspects that the method is biased towards people with higher IQs.

She plans to use the method to choose a sample of 20. Her null hypothesis will be that the sample is a random sample from a population with mean 100 and standard deviation 15. She will use the sample mean $\overline{X}$ as test statistic.

(a) State the distribution of $\overline{X}$.

(b) Will a one-tailed test or a two-tailed test be appropriate?

The researcher will test at the 2% level of significance.

(c) Let Z be the standardised variable corresponding to $\overline{X}$. Find the critical value of Z.

(d) Hence find the critical value of $\overline{X}$ and state the acceptance region in terms of $\overline{X}$.

(e) When the researcher takes the sample she finds that the sample mean $\bar{x}$ is 107.9. What conclusion should she draw?

Test yourself (answers p 130)

1 The lengths of fish of a particular species are normally distributed with a mean of 56 cm and a standard deviation of 4.2 cm. There is a suspicion that, due to overfishing, the mean length of these fish has changed.

A random sample of 50 fish was measured and was found to have a mean length of 54.8 cm.

Investigate, at the 5% level of significance, whether this indicates a change from 56 cm in the mean length of this species of fish.   AQA 2001

2 A random variable X is normally distributed with mean μ and standard deviation 0.8. The null hypothesis $H_0: \mu = 40$ is to be tested against the alternative hypothesis $H_1: \mu \neq 40$ using the 5% level of significance.

The mean, $\overline{X}$, of a random sample of 50 observations is to be used as the test statistic.

(a) Write down

 (i) the distribution of $\overline{X}$ assuming H_0 is true

 (ii) the probability of a Type I error

(b) Calculate the acceptance region for $\overline{X}$, giving its limits to two decimal places.

(c) Explain what is meant by a Type II error.   AQA 2002

3 The lengths of snakes of a particular species are normally distributed with mean 74.6 cm. A zoologist suspects that the snakes of this species that live in a marshland are longer than average. He measures the lengths in cm of a random sample of 10 snakes from the marshland, with these results.

   75.1   77.2   75.2   74.6   73.9   76.1   77.0   75.0   72.8   76.1

Test, at the 5% level of significance, the zoologist's suspicion.

6 Chi-squared tests

In this chapter you will learn
- about the chi-squared distribution
- how use the chi-squared statistic to test goodness of fit and to test for independence in a contingency table

A The chi-squared distribution

Suppose that Z is a continuous random variable with the standard normal distribution.

The distribution of Z is shown in the diagram below.
The area, or probability, for each of the intervals 0–0.5, 0.5–1, 1–1.5, 1.5–2 is shown.
These areas can be found from the table.

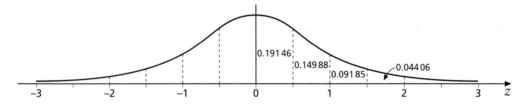

Consider the random variable W, where $W = Z^2$.

We can show the distribution of W by squaring the values of z on the horizontal axis, to give corresponding values of w.

For example, the probability that Z is between 1.5 and 2 is the same as the probability that Z^2, or W, is between 1.5^2 and 2^2, that is between 2.25 and 4.

But there is a complication. When squared, the negative values of z become positive, so the total probability that W is between 2.25 and 4 is the sum of the two shaded areas.

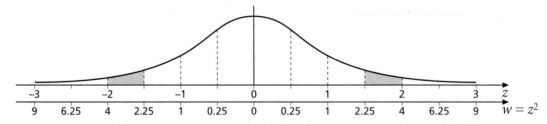

Add the areas on the left-hand part of the graph to those on the right-hand part, so that there is now a single scale for w, or z^2.

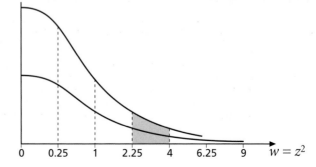

The *w*-scale on the graph is non-uniform. Imagine that it is made uniform in such a way that the area of each strip is not changed.

Some strips are made wider and some narrower, so the height has to be adjusted to make the areas stay the same.

The resulting graph looks like this.

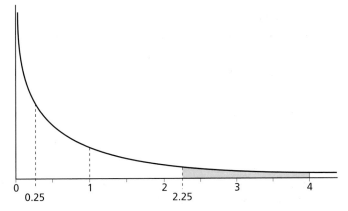

The graph above shows the distribution of Z^2, where Z is a standard normal variable.

This distribution is called the χ^2 (**'chi-squared'**) **distribution** with 1 degree of freedom.

The sum of the squares of n independent normal variables $Z_1^2 + Z_2^2 + \ldots + Z_n^2$ has a distribution called the χ^2-distribution with n degrees of freedom.

This diagram shows some χ^2-distributions with different degrees of freedom (denoted by v, 'nu').

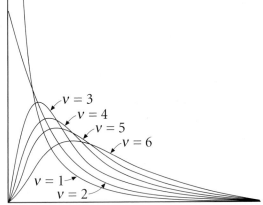

The χ^2-distribution is needed for an important type of hypothesis test that is described in this chapter.

Percentage points of the χ^2-distribution are given in the table on page 115.

The table gives percentage points for both low percentages (0.5%, 1%, 2.5%, 5%, 10%) and high percentages (90%, 95%, 97.5%, 99%, 99.5%).

p	0.005	0.01	0.025	0.05	0.1	0.9	0.95	0.975	0.99	0.995	p
v											v
1	0.00004	0.0002	0.001	0.004	0.016	2.706	3.841	5.024	6.635	7.879	1
2	0.010	0.020	0.051	0.103	0.211	4.605	5.991	7.378	9.210	10.597	2
3	0.072	0.115	0.216	0.352	0.584	6.251	7.815	9.348	11.345	12.838	3
4	0.207	0.297	0.484	0.711	1.064	7.779	9.488	11.143	13.277	14.860	4
5	0.412	0.554	0.831	1.145	1.610	9.236	11.070	12.833	15.086	16.750	5

B Testing goodness of fit (answers p 131)

A student is playing a game with a dice and suspects that the dice is biased towards the score 1, because this score seems to come up more often than it should. She decides to test the dice by rolling it 60 times and counting the number of times the score 1 comes up and the number of times another score comes up. Here are her results.

Score	1	other
Frequency	15	45

The student's null hypothesis is that the dice is not biased towards 1, so that the probability of scoring 1 is $\frac{1}{6}$. Under this hypothesis, the expected frequency for score 1 is 10 and for other scores 50.

In order to test the null hypothesis against the alternative hypothesis that the dice **is** biased towards 1, the observed frequencies need to be compared with the expected frequencies. For this a suitable test statistic is needed.

The observed frequency (O) and the expected frequency (E) for each outcome are shown in this table.

Score	1	other
Observed frequency (O)	15	45
Expected frequency (E)	10	50

B1 The student's first idea is to find the difference ($O - E$) for each outcome and add the results. Why will this not give a measure of how far the observed and expected frequencies differ overall?

In order to arrive at a useful test statistic, three steps are taken:

- Each difference ($O - E$) is squared to give $(O - E)^2$, so that there are no negative values.

- Each value of $(O - E)^2$ is divided by the value of E to give $\dfrac{(O - E)^2}{E}$.

- The values of $\dfrac{(O - E)^2}{E}$ are summed to give the test statistic $\sum \dfrac{(O - E)^2}{E}$.

For the dice situation described above, the distribution of this test statistic can be shown to be approximately a χ^2-distribution with 1 degree of freedom. An explanation is given on page 108.

Although there are two values of O, there is only one degree of freedom. This is because when one value of O is known, the other follows automatically because the two values must add up to 60.

To test the null hypothesis that the dice is not biased towards 1, we need to decide the level of significance and then determine the critical region.

Suppose the level of significance is 5%.

If the null hypothesis is true, then we would expect the values of O to be close to the values of E, so the value of the test statistic $\sum \frac{(O-E)^2}{E}$ would be low.

High values of the test statistic are evidence against the null hypothesis, so we use a one-tailed test with a critical value that has 5% of the distribution above it.

From the table, the 95% percentage point of the χ^2-distribution with $v = 1$ is 3.841. This the critical value.

0.05	0.1	0.9	0.95	0.975	0.99	0.995	p
							v
0.004	0.016	2.706	(3.841)	5.024	6.635	7.879	1
0.103	0.211	4.605	5.991	7.378	9.210	10.597	2

$\sum \frac{(O-E)^2}{E}$ is called the 'χ^2-statistic'. If its value for a particular set of data turns out to be greater than the critical value, then we will reject the null hypothesis at the 5% level of significance.

B2 (a) Calculate the value of the χ^2-statistic for the student's dice scores data.

(b) Is this value in the critical region?

(c) State the conclusion of the test.

The test that you have carried out is an example of a test of 'goodness of fit'. It is a test of whether the observed data fits the values predicted by the null hypothesis.

Another student has a dice that she thinks may be unfair and decides to roll it 120 times and record every score that she gets. Here are her results.

Score	1	2	3	4	5	6
Frequency	30	34	15	17	11	13

The student's null hypothesis is that the dice is fair, so that the distribution of the six possible scores is uniform. Under this hypothesis, the expected frequency for each score is 20. The values of O and E are shown in this table.

Score	1	2	3	4	5	6
Observed frequency (O)	30	34	15	17	11	13
Expected frequency (E)	20	20	20	20	20	20

In this case the test statistic has, approximately, the χ^2-distribution with 5 degrees of freedom. This is because the six values of O are not all independent: they must add up to the same total as the expected frequencies, 120. When five of the values are given, the value of the sixth follows automatically.

So for this data, $\sum \frac{(O-E)^2}{E}$ has approximately the χ^2-distribution with $v = 5$.

From the table, the 95% percentage point of the χ^2-distribution with $v = 5$ is 11.07. This is the critical value for the 5% level of significance.

0.05	0.1	0.9	0.95	0.975	0.99	0.995	p
							v
0.004	0.016	2.706	3.841	5.024	6.635	7.879	1
0.103	0.211	4.605	5.991	7.378	9.210	10.597	2
0.352	0.584	6.251	7.815	9.348	11.345	12.838	3
0.711	1.064	7.779	9.488	11.143	13.277	14.860	4
1.145	1.610	9.236	(11.070)	12.833	15.086	16.750	5

B3 Calculate the value of the χ^2-statistic for the dice scores data above and state the conclusion of the test.

In each dice scores example, the student decided how many times to roll the dice before the data was collected. So it was possible to calculate the expected frequencies under the null hypothesis before the observed frequencies became known.

In the next example, no decision is made in advance about the size of the sample.

A librarian claims that more books are borrowed on certain weekdays. She records the number of books borrowed each day during one week.

Day	Mon	Tue	Wed	Thu	Fri
Books borrowed	68	80	77	93	98

The hypotheses are

H_0: Books are borrowed in equal numbers on all days.
H_1: More books are borrowed on certain days.

It is obvious that in the week for which the data is given, the numbers borrowed on Thursday and Friday were much larger than on the other three days. But this was just one week. The hypotheses are about weekdays in general and we have to decide whether a week with numbers as unequal as this one is so unlikely to happen under hypothesis H_0 that we would reject the hypothesis.

In the particular week recorded, the total number of books borrowed was 416. To work out expected frequencies under H_0 we have to imagine that the 416 books are redistributed equally between the five days, giving an expected frequency of 83.2 each day. (It does not matter that this is not a whole number.)

To help get the idea that the actual numbers above represent only one possible outcome, think of the data table with the expected frequencies filled in but awaiting observed frequencies, like this.

Day	Mon	Tue	Wed	Thu	Fri
Observed frequency (O)					
Expected frequency (E)	83.2	83.2	83.2	83.2	83.2

The expected frequencies add up to 416, so whatever frequencies are observed must also add up to 416. So if any four are given, the fifth follows automatically.

So although the total number of books, unlike the total number of dice throws, was not fixed in advance, the number of degrees of freedom is still one less than the number of observed frequencies. This is because the total number of books has been used to work out the expected frequencies and so is fixed.

B4 (a) Find the 95% percentage point for the χ^2-distribution with $v = 4$. This is the critical value for a test of H_0 at the 5% significance level.

(b) Find the value of the χ^2-statistic for the librarian's data.

(c) State the conclusion of the test.

K The goodness of fit between a set of k observed frequencies O and expected frequencies E can be tested using the test statistic $\sum \dfrac{(O-E)^2}{E}$ which has, approximately, the χ^2-distribution with $k-1$ degrees of freedom.

For the approximation to be valid, each value of O must be greater than 5.

K If a value of O is less than 6, some categories in the data must be combined to make the value of O large enough. For example,

Score	1	2	3	4	5	6
Frequency	14	12	11	7	4	2

becomes

Score	1	2	3	4	5 or 6
Frequency	14	12	11	7	6

Example 1

A biologist has developed a theory that four varieties of plant should occur in the proportions $1:3:3:1$.

She counts the numbers of each variety growing in a large field, with these results.

Variety	A	B	C	D
Frequency	12	51	74	17

Test, at the 5% significance level, the hypothesis that these results are consistent with the biologist's theory.

Solution

The hypotheses are H_0: The ratio of the frequencies is $1:3:3:1$.

 H_1: The ratio of the frequencies is not $1:3:3:1$.

The total number of plants counted is 154.

Based on this total, the expected frequencies are $\frac{1}{8}$ of 154, $\frac{3}{8}$ of 154, $\frac{3}{8}$ of 154, $\frac{1}{8}$ of 154, that is 19.25, 57.75, 57.75, 19.25.

Given a total expected frequency of 154, the four observed frequencies of any sample must add up to 154, so there are 3 degrees of freedom.

From the table, the 95% percentage point of the χ^2-distribution with $v = 3$ is 7.815.

For the given data, χ^2-statistic $= \sum \dfrac{(O-E)^2}{E}$

$$= \frac{(12-19.25)^2}{19.25} + \frac{(51-57.75)^2}{57.75} + \frac{(74-57.75)^2}{57.75} + \frac{(17-19.25)^2}{19.25}$$
$$= 8.355 \text{ (to 3 d.p.)}$$

This value is greater than the critical value, so reject H_0.

Conclusion: At the 5% level of significance the data is inconsistent with the theory.

Exercise B (answers p 131)

1 A student counts the number of sweets of different colours in several packets, with the overall results shown in the table.

Colour	Red	Yellow	Green	Orange
Frequency	20	14	11	15

Test, at the 5% significance level, whether there is evidence that some colours are more common than others.

2 A quality controller in a factory takes a daily sample of 100 items and counts the number of defective items in the sample. Over a period of six days the numbers of defective items were as follows.

Day	1	2	3	4	5	6
No of defective items	12	14	6	13	8	10

Test at the 5% significance level whether these results are consistent with the hypothesis that the probability that an item is defective is constant from day to day.

3 The principles of genetics were first put forward by the Austrian botanist Gregor Mendel in 1865. He experimented with pea plants to test his theories. According to his theory, plants of a certain type should produce peas that are round and yellow (RY), wrinkled and yellow (WY), round and green (RG) and wrinkled and green (WG) in the ratio $9:3:3:1$.

In an experiment 100 of the pea plants are grown and the type of peas produced by them is noted.

Type	RY	WY	RG	WG
Frequency	55	20	16	9

(a) State appropriate hypotheses H_0 and H_1.

(b) Test at the 5% significance level whether the data supports Mendel's theory.

4 A canteen supervisor thinks that more students have a school lunch on some days than others. In one particular week the numbers recorded were as follows.

Day	Mon	Tue	Wed	Thu	Fri
Number	355	320	344	314	327

Test at the 10% significance level whether there is evidence that the numbers are not the same for every day of the week.

5 Until recently, the numbers of customers using each of four supermarkets A, B, C, D have been consistently in the ratio $6:5:3:1$.

Supermarket C introduces a range of cheap products. In the week after this, the numbers of customers in the four supermarkets are as follows.

Supermarket	A	B	C	D
No of customers	2898	2423	1625	516

Test at the 5% significance level whether the ratio of customers using the four supermarkets has changed.

6 In a certain constituency, at the last election, Labour won 40% of the votes cast, Conservative 35% and Liberal Democrat 25%. Another election is now taking place. An exit poll of a random sample of 500 voters gives the following numbers:

Labour 188,   Conservative 164,   Liberal Democrat 148

Test at the 5% significance level whether there is evidence that the proportions voting for the three parties have changed since the last election.

C Contingency tables (answers p 132)

A travel agent sells 'weekend breaks' to customers. A break can be taken in a city or in the country or at the seaside. The travel agent would like to know whether customers' satisfaction or dissatisfaction is linked to where they spend their break. So he sends a questionnaire to a random sample of people who have recently had a weekend break. Here are the results.

	City	Country	Seaside
Satisfied	18	16	8
Dissatisfied	16	8	14

This is an example of a **contingency table** – a two-way table in which the entries are frequencies.

We shall need the totals of the rows and columns. These are shown below, together with the overall total.

	City	Country	Seaside	Total
Satisfied	18	16	8	42
Dissatisfied	16	8	14	38
Total	34	24	22	80

The travel agent wants to know whether there is a link between where people go and their satisfaction. His null hypothesis is that there is no link, or in other words that the probabilities of being satisfied and of being dissatisfied are the same for all three destinations.

Of the 80 people in the sample, 42 were satisfied. From this we estimate that, in the population as a whole, the probability of being satisfied is $\frac{42}{80}$.

There were 34 people who went to a city. Under the null hypothesis we would expect $\frac{42}{80}$ of these to be satisfied.

So the expected number of satisfied city goers is $\frac{42}{80} \times 34 = 17.85$.

We can build up a table of expected frequencies for a group of 80 people under the null hypothesis that 'satisfied/dissatisfied' are independent of 'city/country/seaside'.

This number is $\frac{42 \times 34}{80}$.

	City	Country	Seaside	Total
Satisfied	17.85			(42)
Dissatisfied				38
Total	(34)	24	22	80

C1 (a) Show that if the null hypothesis is true, the expected number of satisfied country goers is 12.6.

(b) Find the expected number of dissatisfied seaside goers.

The completed table is as follows.

Expected frequencies

	City	Country	Seaside	Total
Satisfied	17.85	12.60	11.55	42
Dissatisfied	16.15	11.40	10.45	38
Total	34	24	22	**80**

We now need to find the number of degrees of freedom. We note that the expected frequencies have been based on the row and column totals. So whatever numbers appear in the table of observed frequencies, the row and column totals are fixed.

The table below shows that when two observed frequencies, such as those marked √, are known, the others, marked ×, are automatically determined.

Observed frequencies

	City	Country	Seaside	Total
Satisfied	√	√	×	42
Dissatisfied	×	×	×	38
Total	34	24	22	**80**

So the number of degrees of freedom is 2.

C2 (a) Find the 95% percentage point of the χ^2-distribution with $v = 2$. This is the critical value for a test at the 5% level of significance.

(b) Find the value of $\dfrac{(O - E)^2}{E}$ for each of the six frequencies in the travel agent's data and hence the value of the χ^2-statistic $\sum \dfrac{(O - E)^2}{E}$.

(c) Is there evidence at the 5% significance level that customer satisfaction is linked to where customers go for their break?

If a contingency table has, say, 3 rows and 5 columns, the pattern of ticks and crosses is as shown here.

There are $2 \times 4 = 8$ degrees of freedom.

√	√	√	√	×
√	√	√	√	×
×	×	×	×	×

In a contingency table with r rows and c columns, there are $(r - 1)(c - 1)$ degrees of freedom.

Yates's correction

In the case of a 2 by 2 contingency table, there is only 1 degree of freedom. The English statistician Frank Yates (1902–1994) found that in this case instead of the expression $(O - E)^2$ it is better to use the expression $(|O - E| - 0.5)^2$.

For example, if in a 2 by 2 table one of the observed frequencies is 27 and its expected value is 31, then for this frequency

$$(|O - E| - 0.5)^2 = (|27 - 31| - 0.5)^2 = (4 - 0.5)^2 = 3.5^2 = 12.25.$$

The test statistic for a 2 by 2 table is $\sum \dfrac{(|O - E| - 0.5)^2}{E}$.

Otherwise, the process is the same as for other contingency tables.

Example 2

In order to test a drug which is said to alleviate colds, a random sample of patients were given a high dose, or a low dose, or a pill that contained none of the drug at all. The patients were not told which of the three treatments they were given. Their reactions are given in this contingency table.

	Helped	Harmed	No effect
High dose	10	10	15
Low dose	14	8	9
Zero dose	16	7	19

Test, at the 5% level of significance, the hypothesis that the dosage has no effect on the patient's reaction.

Solution

The hypotheses are H_0: reaction is independent of dosage
H_1: reaction is not independent of dosage

Row and column totals are shown here.

	Helped	Harmed	No effect	
High dose	10	10	15	35
Low dose	14	8	9	31
Zero dose	16	7	19	42
	40	25	43	108

If H_0 is true, the probability of each reaction is the same whatever the dosage.

An estimate of the overall probability that a patient is helped is $\frac{40}{108}$.

So out of the 35 high-dose patients, $\frac{40}{108} \times 35 = 12.96$ are expected to be helped.

Other expected frequencies are calculated in the same way. The table is shown here.

	Helped	Harmed	No effect
High dose	12.96	8.10	13.94
Low dose	11.48	7.18	12.34
Zero dose	15.56	9.72	16.72

There are 3 rows and 3 columns, so $r = 3$ and $c = 3$.
The number of degrees of freedom is $(r-1)(c-1) = 2 \times 2 = 4$.

From the percentage points table, the 95% percentage point of the χ^2-distribution with $v = 4$ is 9.488.

$$\chi^2\text{-statistic} = \sum \frac{(O-E)^2}{E} = \frac{(10-12.96)^2}{12.96} + \frac{(10-8.10)^2}{8.10} + \dots + \frac{(19-16.72)^2}{16.72} = 3.84 \text{ (to 3 s.f.)}$$

The value of the χ^2-statistic is less than the critical value 9.488, so accept H_0.

Conclusion: There is insufficient evidence, at the 5% level of significance, of a link between dosage and the patient's reaction.

Example 3

A random sample of music students were entered for a music exam in which the result could be Distinction, Pass or Fail. The table shows the results for boys and girls. Test, at the 5% significance level, the hypothesis that there is no link between gender and exam result.

	Distinction	Pass	Fail
Boys	4	21	20
Girls	6	42	13

Solution

One of the cells in the table has a frequency less than 6. This is too low for a χ^2-test to be accurate, so the columns 'Distinction' and 'Pass' must be combined.

	Distinction or Pass	Fail	Total
Boys	25	20	45
Girls	48	13	61
Total	73	33	**106**

The null hypothesis is that exam result and gender are independent. Under this hypothesis, the expected frequencies are $\dfrac{73 \times 45}{106} = 30.99$, etc.

	Distinction or Pass	Fail
Boys	30.99	14.01
Girls	42.01	18.99

The number of degrees of freedom is $(2-1) \times (2-1) = 1$.

The 95% percentage point of the χ^2-distribution with $v = 1$ is 3.841.

As the table is now 2 by 2, Yates's correction must be used.

$$\chi^2\text{-statistic} = \sum \frac{(|O - E| - 0.5)^2}{E} = \frac{(|25 - 30.99| - 0.5)^2}{30.99} + \ldots = 5.43$$

This is greater than the critical value 3.841 so reject H_0.

Conclusion: There is evidence, at the 5% level, of a link between gender and result.

Very low values of the χ^2-statistic

So far we have looked at a χ^2-test as a way of testing whether observed frequencies are close enough to expected values for the null hypothesis to be accepted. So the value of the χ^2-statistic has been generally quite high and the question has been whether it is high enough to reject the null hypothesis.

A very low value of the statistic indicates an extremely good fit, so good in fact that we might suspect that the data may not be from a genuine random sample.

For example, if an ordinary dice is rolled 120 times, the expected frequency of each score is 20. Suppose we are told that the observed frequencies are 21, 20, 17, 22, 19, 21.

The value of the χ^2-statistic $= \dfrac{(21 - 20)^2}{20} + \dfrac{(20 - 20)^2}{20} + \ldots + \dfrac{(21 - 20)^2}{20} = 0.8$

This is less than the 5% percentage point of the χ^2-distribution with 5 d.f., which is 1.145.

In fact it is even less than the 2.5% percentage point, which is 0.831.
In other words, the probability of getting a set of frequencies as close as this to the expected value is less than 2.5%.

This raises the suspicion that the data may have been 'cooked' to fit the expected frequencies. It does not prove that this has been done, but it raises the question.

Exercise C (answers p 132)

1 Fruit trees are susceptible to a certain disease. Three treatments are possible: do nothing, cut off affected branches, or spray with a chemical.
Three outcomes are possible: the tree dies within a year or lives for between one and two years or lives for over two years.

This contingency table shows the results of treating a random sample of trees.

	Lived < 1 year	Lived 1–2 years	Lived > 2 years
No treatment	48	32	20
Branches cut	18	34	38
Sprayed	8	21	31

Test, at the 5% significance level, the hypothesis that the outcomes are independent of the treatments.

2 A company making crisps wishes to know whether a preference for strong or mild flavours is linked to age. They record the preferences of a random sample of people, with the results shown here.

	Strong	Mild
Age under 30	58	42
Age 30 or over	46	51

Test at the 1% significance level whether there is evidence of an association between preference and age.

3 A teacher wishes to test his theory that male and female students tend to make different kinds of error in their written work. He collects a random sample of students' 500-word essays and counts the number of errors in spelling, punctuation and grammar in each essay. His results are shown in the table below.

	Spelling	Punctuation	Grammar
Male	34	17	5
Female	14	16	4

State the null hypothesis and test it at the 5% level of significance.

Key points

- The goodness of fit between a set of k observed frequencies O and expected frequencies E can be tested using the test statistic $\sum \dfrac{(O-E)^2}{E}$ which has, approximately, the χ^2-distribution with $k-1$ degrees of freedom. (p 98)

- If a value of O is less than 6, some categories in the data must be combined to make a value of O that is 6 or greater. (p 99)

- In a contingency table with r rows and c columns, there are $(r-1)(c-1)$ degrees of freedom. (p 102)

- The test statistic for a 2 by 2 table is $\sum \dfrac{(|O-E|-0.5)^2}{E}$. (p 102)

Mixed questions (answers p 133)

1 The prisoners in a high-security jail are placed into three categories: short stay, medium stay and long stay. The frequency with which the prisoners receive mail is monitored and the results recorded in the table below.

	Length of stay in prison			
	Short	Medium	Long	
Regular mail	40	24	8	72
Occasional mail	12	18	15	45
No mail	13	27	22	62
	65	69	45	179

Stating your null and alternative hypotheses, investigate, at the 1% level of significance, the claim that there is no association between length of stay in prison and the frequency with which prisoners receive mail.

AQA 2002

2 Baljeet's parents want to choose a school for her to attend in order to pursue her sixth-form studies. They have a choice of sending her to one of two schools, X or Y. To help them make an informed choice, they decide to look at the numbers of A, B, C and D grades achieved last year by each school. These are tabulated below.

	Examination grades				
	A	B	C	D	Total
School X	52	34	16	18	120
School Y	114	58	62	46	280
Total	166	92	78	64	400

Stating the null hypothesis, carry out a χ^2-test at the 5% level of significance to determine whether there is an association between the schools and the numbers of A, B, C and D grades achieved.

AQA 2004

3 An amateur weather forecaster wishes to assess whether there is any association between the midday temperatures that she predicts and the actual temperatures recorded. She takes a random sample of previous forecasts and notes whether the predicted temperature was below, at or above normal, and whether the actual temperature was below, at or above normal. The sample data is shown in the table below.

		Actual temperature		
		Below normal	Normal	Above normal
Predicted temperature	Below normal	44	17	12
	Normal	25	35	16
	Above normal	8	19	22

Stating the null hypothesis, test at the 1% level of significance whether there is any association between the predicted and actual temperatures.

4 In a study of preferences for colour schemes, a student asks a random sample of 17-year-olds to choose between four colour schemes for a room. The schemes, A, B, C and D, range from mostly white, through lighter and darker pastel shades to bold primary colours. The student records males' and females' preferences, with the following results.

	A	B	C	D
Males	14	10	16	19
Females	18	24	12	7

Test at the 10% level of significance the hypothesis that there is no link between gender and preference.

Test yourself (answers p 134)

1 A student has designed a device that is intended to generate random digits from 0 to 9. The device was set to generate 500 'random' digits. The results were as follows.

Digit	0	1	2	3	4	5	6	7	8	9
Frequency	54	52	44	50	41	56	53	39	57	54

Test at the 5% level of significance the hypothesis that each of the ten digits is equally likely.

2 For her 17th birthday present, Susan wishes to have a course of driving lessons. In an attempt to select the best driving school in the area, her parents compare recent test results of two schools, A and B.

These test results are tabulated below.

	School A	School B
Pass	120	100
Fail	24	36

Stating the null hypothesis, use a χ^2-test at the 5% level of significance to determine whether there is an association between test results and driving school. AQA 2002

3 The results of a recent police survey of traffic travelling on motorways produced information about the genders of drivers and the speeds, S miles per hour, of their vehicles, as tabulated below.

	Speed of vehicles		
	$S \leq 70$	$70 < S \leq 90$	$S > 90$
Male	17	40	70
Female	30	25	18

Stating null and alternative hypotheses, investigate, at the 1% level of significance, the claim that there is no association between the gender of the driver and the speed of the vehicle. AQA 2002

Why the distribution of the test statistic $\sum \dfrac{(O-E)^2}{E}$ is approximately χ^2

The case where it is suspected that a dice is biased towards score 1 is a case of the following situation.

Suppose n independent trials are carried out in which each trial has two possible outcomes A or B, with probabilities p and $1-p$ respectively.

Let O_1 be the number of times A occurs and O_2 be the number of times B occurs.

Then O_1 has the binomial distribution with parameters n, p.
Similarly, O_2 has the binomial distribution with parameters n, $1-p$.

So O_1 has expected value np and variance $np(1-p)$.

Similarly O_2 has expected value $n(1-p)$ and variance $n(1-p)(1-(1-p)) = np(1-p)$.

So $\displaystyle\sum \frac{(O-E)^2}{E} = \frac{(O_1-np)^2}{np} + \frac{(O_2-n(1-p))^2}{n(1-p)}$

But $O_1 + O_2 = n$, because there are n trials altogether.

So $O_2 - n(1-p) = n - O_1 - n + np = np - O_1$.

So the numerator of both fractions in the expression above is $(O_1 - np)^2$.

So $\displaystyle\sum \frac{(O-E)^2}{E} = \frac{(O_1-np)^2}{n}\left(\frac{1}{p}+\frac{1}{1-p}\right) = \frac{(O_1-np)^2}{np(1-p)}$

It can be shown that if X has a binomial distribution, then the standardised variable
$\dfrac{X-\mu}{\sigma} = \dfrac{X-np}{\sqrt{np(1-p)}}$ has approximately the standard normal distribution when
n is sufficiently large.

So, for sufficiently large n, $\dfrac{(O_1-np)^2}{np(1-p)}$ is the square of a standard normal variable and
thus has the χ^2-distribution with 1 degree of freedom.

In general it can be shown that for k random variables $O_1, O_2, \ldots, O_k$ with expected values $np_1, np_2, \ldots, np_k$, the distribution of

$$\frac{(O_1-np_1)^2}{np_1} + \frac{(O_2-np_2)^2}{np_2} + \ldots + \frac{(O_k-np_k)^2}{np_k}$$

is approximately the χ^2-distribution with $k-1$ degrees of freedom.

Tables

Cumulative Poisson distribution function

The tabulated value is $P(X \le x)$, where X has a Poisson distribution with mean λ.

λ	0.10	0.20	0.30	0.40	0.50	0.60	0.70	0.80	0.90	1.0	1.2	1.4	1.6	1.8	λ
x															x
0	0.9048	0.8187	0.7408	0.6703	0.6065	0.5488	0.4966	0.4493	0.4066	0.3679	0.3012	0.2466	0.2019	0.1653	0
1	0.9953	0.9825	0.9631	0.9384	0.9098	0.8781	0.8442	0.8088	0.7725	0.7358	0.6626	0.5918	0.5249	0.4628	1
2	0.9998	0.9989	0.9964	0.9921	0.9856	0.9769	0.9659	0.9526	0.9371	0.9197	0.8795	0.8335	0.7834	0.7306	2
3	1.0000	0.9999	0.9997	0.9992	0.9982	0.9966	0.9942	0.9909	0.9865	0.9810	0.9662	0.9463	0.9212	0.8913	3
4		1.0000	1.0000	0.9999	0.9998	0.9996	0.9992	0.9986	0.9977	0.9963	0.9923	0.9857	0.9763	0.9636	4
5				1.0000	1.0000	1.0000	0.9999	0.9998	0.9997	0.9994	0.9985	0.9968	0.9940	0.9896	5
6							1.0000	1.0000	1.0000	0.9999	0.9997	0.9994	0.9987	0.9974	6
7										1.0000	1.0000	0.9999	0.9997	0.9994	7
8												1.0000	1.0000	0.9999	8
9														1.0000	9

λ	2.0	2.2	2.4	2.6	2.8	3.0	3.2	3.4	3.6	3.8	4.0	4.5	5.0	5.5	λ
x															x
0	0.1353	0.1108	0.0907	0.0743	0.0608	0.0498	0.0408	0.0334	0.0273	0.0224	0.0183	0.0111	0.0067	0.0041	0
1	0.4060	0.3546	0.3084	0.2674	0.2311	0.1991	0.1712	0.1468	0.1257	0.1074	0.0916	0.0611	0.0404	0.0266	1
2	0.6767	0.6227	0.5697	0.5184	0.4695	0.4232	0.3799	0.3397	0.3027	0.2689	0.2381	0.1736	0.1247	0.0884	2
3	0.8571	0.8194	0.7787	0.7360	0.6919	0.6472	0.6025	0.5584	0.5152	0.4735	0.4335	0.3423	0.2650	0.2017	3
4	0.9473	0.9275	0.9041	0.8774	0.8477	0.8153	0.7806	0.7442	0.7064	0.6678	0.6288	0.5321	0.4405	0.3575	4
5	0.9834	0.9751	0.9643	0.9510	0.9349	0.9161	0.8946	0.8705	0.8441	0.8156	0.7851	0.7029	0.6160	0.5289	5
6	0.9955	0.9925	0.9884	0.9828	0.9756	0.9665	0.9554	0.9421	0.9267	0.9091	0.8893	0.8311	0.7622	0.6860	6
7	0.9989	0.9980	0.9967	0.9947	0.9919	0.9881	0.9832	0.9769	0.9692	0.9599	0.9489	0.9134	0.8666	0.8095	7
8	0.9998	0.9995	0.9991	0.9985	0.9976	0.9962	0.9943	0.9917	0.9883	0.9840	0.9786	0.9597	0.9319	0.8944	8
9	1.0000	0.9999	0.9998	0.9996	0.9993	0.9989	0.9982	0.9973	0.9960	0.9942	0.9919	0.9829	0.9682	0.9462	9
10		1.0000	1.0000	0.9999	0.9998	0.9997	0.9995	0.9992	0.9987	0.9981	0.9972	0.9933	0.9863	0.9747	10
11				1.0000	1.0000	0.9999	0.9999	0.9998	0.9996	0.9994	0.9991	0.9976	0.9945	0.9890	11
12						1.0000	1.0000	0.9999	0.9999	0.9998	0.9997	0.9992	0.9980	0.9955	12
13								1.0000	1.0000	1.0000	0.9999	0.9997	0.9993	0.9983	13
14											1.0000	0.9999	0.9998	0.9994	14
15												1.0000	0.9999	0.9998	15
16													1.0000	0.9999	16
17														1.0000	17

λ	6.0	6.5	7.0	7.5	8.0	8.5	9.0	9.5	10.0	11.0	12.0	13.0	14.0	15.0	λ
x															x
0	0.0025	0.0015	0.0009	0.0006	0.0003	0.0002	0.0001	0.0001	0.0000	0.0000	0.0000	0.0000	0.0000	0.0000	0
1	0.0174	0.0113	0.0073	0.0047	0.0030	0.0019	0.0012	0.0008	0.0005	0.0002	0.0001	0.0000	0.0000	0.0000	1
2	0.0620	0.0430	0.0296	0.0203	0.0138	0.0093	0.0062	0.0042	0.0028	0.0012	0.0005	0.0002	0.0001	0.0000	2
3	0.1512	0.1118	0.0818	0.0591	0.0424	0.0301	0.0212	0.0149	0.0103	0.0049	0.0023	0.0011	0.0005	0.0002	3
4	0.2851	0.2237	0.1730	0.1321	0.0996	0.0744	0.0550	0.0403	0.0293	0.0151	0.0076	0.0037	0.0018	0.0009	4
5	0.4457	0.3690	0.3007	0.2414	0.1912	0.1496	0.1157	0.0885	0.0671	0.0375	0.0203	0.0107	0.0055	0.0028	5
6	0.6063	0.5265	0.4497	0.3782	0.3134	0.2562	0.2068	0.1649	0.1301	0.0786	0.0458	0.0259	0.0142	0.0076	6
7	0.7440	0.6728	0.5987	0.5246	0.4530	0.3856	0.3239	0.2687	0.2202	0.1432	0.0895	0.0540	0.0316	0.0180	7
8	0.8472	0.7916	0.7291	0.6620	0.5925	0.5231	0.4557	0.3918	0.3328	0.2320	0.1550	0.0998	0.0621	0.0374	8
9	0.9161	0.8774	0.8305	0.7764	0.7166	0.6530	0.5874	0.5218	0.4579	0.3405	0.2424	0.1658	0.1094	0.0699	9
10	0.9574	0.9332	0.9015	0.8622	0.8159	0.7634	0.7060	0.6453	0.5830	0.4599	0.3472	0.2517	0.1757	0.1185	10
11	0.9799	0.9661	0.9467	0.9208	0.8881	0.8487	0.8030	0.7520	0.6968	0.5793	0.4616	0.3532	0.2600	0.1848	11
12	0.9912	0.9840	0.9730	0.9573	0.9362	0.9091	0.8758	0.8364	0.7916	0.6887	0.5760	0.4631	0.3585	0.2676	12
13	0.9964	0.9929	0.9872	0.9784	0.9658	0.9486	0.9261	0.8981	0.8645	0.7813	0.6815	0.5730	0.4644	0.3632	13
14	0.9986	0.9970	0.9943	0.9897	0.9827	0.9726	0.9585	0.9400	0.9165	0.8540	0.7720	0.6751	0.5704	0.4657	14
15	0.9995	0.9988	0.9976	0.9954	0.9918	0.9862	0.9780	0.9665	0.9513	0.9074	0.8444	0.7636	0.6694	0.5681	15
16	0.9998	0.9996	0.9990	0.9980	0.9963	0.9934	0.9889	0.9823	0.9730	0.9441	0.8987	0.8355	0.7559	0.6641	16
17	0.9999	0.9998	0.9996	0.9992	0.9984	0.9970	0.9947	0.9911	0.9857	0.9678	0.9370	0.8905	0.8272	0.7489	17
18	1.0000	0.9999	0.9999	0.9997	0.9993	0.9987	0.9976	0.9957	0.9928	0.9823	0.9626	0.9302	0.8826	0.8195	18
19		1.0000	1.0000	0.9999	0.9997	0.9995	0.9989	0.9980	0.9965	0.9907	0.9787	0.9573	0.9235	0.8752	19
20				1.0000	0.9999	0.9998	0.9996	0.9991	0.9984	0.9953	0.9884	0.9750	0.9521	0.9170	20
21					1.0000	0.9999	0.9998	0.9996	0.9993	0.9977	0.9939	0.9859	0.9712	0.9469	21
22						1.0000	0.9999	0.9999	0.9997	0.9990	0.9970	0.9924	0.9833	0.9673	22
23							1.0000	0.9999	0.9999	0.9995	0.9985	0.9960	0.9907	0.9805	23
24								1.0000	1.0000	0.9998	0.9993	0.9980	0.9950	0.9888	24
25										0.9999	0.9997	0.9990	0.9974	0.9938	25
26										1.0000	0.9999	0.9995	0.9987	0.9967	26
27											0.9999	0.9998	0.9994	0.9983	27
28											1.0000	0.9999	0.9997	0.9991	28
29												1.0000	0.9999	0.9996	29
30													0.9999	0.9998	30
31													1.0000	0.9999	31
32														1.0000	32

Normal distribution function

The table gives the probability, p, that a normally distributed random variable Z, with mean = 0 and variance = 1, is less than or equal to z.

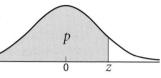

z	0.00	0.01	0.02	0.03	0.04	0.05	0.06	0.07	0.08	0.09	z
0.0	0.50000	0.50399	0.50798	0.51197	0.51595	0.51994	0.52392	0.52790	0.53188	0.53586	**0.0**
0.1	0.53983	0.54380	0.54776	0.55172	0.55567	0.55962	0.56356	0.56749	0.57142	0.57535	**0.1**
0.2	0.57926	0.58317	0.58706	0.59095	0.59483	0.59871	0.60257	0.60642	0.61026	0.61409	**0.2**
0.3	0.61791	0.62172	0.62552	0.62930	0.63307	0.63683	0.64058	0.64431	0.64803	0.65173	**0.3**
0.4	0.65542	0.65910	0.66276	0.66640	0.67003	0.67364	0.67724	0.68082	0.68439	0.68793	**0.4**
0.5	0.69146	0.69497	0.69847	0.70194	0.70540	0.70884	0.71226	0.71566	0.71904	0.72240	**0.5**
0.6	0.72575	0.72907	0.73237	0.73565	0.73891	0.74215	0.74537	0.74857	0.75175	0.75490	**0.6**
0.7	0.75804	0.76115	0.76424	0.76730	0.77035	0.77337	0.77637	0.77935	0.78230	0.78524	**0.7**
0.8	0.78814	0.79103	0.79389	0.79673	0.79955	0.80234	0.80511	0.80785	0.81057	0.81327	**0.8**
0.9	0.81594	0.81859	0.82121	0.82381	0.82639	0.82894	0.83147	0.83398	0.83646	0.83891	**0.9**
1.0	0.84134	0.84375	0.84614	0.84849	0.85083	0.85314	0.85543	0.85769	0.85993	0.86214	**1.0**
1.1	0.86433	0.86650	0.86864	0.87076	0.87286	0.87493	0.87698	0.87900	0.88100	0.88298	**1.1**
1.2	0.88493	0.88686	0.88877	0.89065	0.89251	0.89435	0.89617	0.89796	0.89973	0.90147	**1.2**
1.3	0.90320	0.90490	0.90658	0.90824	0.90988	0.91149	0.91309	0.91466	0.91621	0.91774	**1.3**
1.4	0.91924	0.92073	0.92220	0.92364	0.92507	0.92647	0.92785	0.92922	0.93056	0.93189	**1.4**
1.5	0.93319	0.93448	0.93574	0.93699	0.93822	0.93943	0.94062	0.94179	0.94295	0.94408	**1.5**
1.6	0.94520	0.94630	0.94738	0.94845	0.94950	0.95053	0.95154	0.95254	0.95352	0.95449	**1.6**
1.7	0.95543	0.95637	0.95728	0.95818	0.95907	0.95994	0.96080	0.96164	0.96246	0.96327	**1.7**
1.8	0.96407	0.96485	0.96562	0.96638	0.96712	0.96784	0.96856	0.96926	0.96995	0.97062	**1.8**
1.9	0.97128	0.97193	0.97257	0.97320	0.97381	0.97441	0.97500	0.97558	0.97615	0.97670	**1.9**
2.0	0.97725	0.97778	0.97831	0.97882	0.97932	0.97982	0.98030	0.98077	0.98124	0.98169	**2.0**
2.1	0.98214	0.98257	0.98300	0.98341	0.98382	0.98422	0.98461	0.98500	0.98537	0.98574	**2.1**
2.2	0.98610	0.98645	0.98679	0.98713	0.98745	0.98778	0.98809	0.98840	0.98870	0.98899	**2.2**
2.3	0.98928	0.98956	0.98983	0.99010	0.99036	0.99061	0.99086	0.99111	0.99134	0.99158	**2.3**
2.4	0.99180	0.99202	0.99224	0.99245	0.99266	0.99286	0.99305	0.99324	0.99343	0.99361	**2.4**
2.5	0.99379	0.99396	0.99413	0.99430	0.99446	0.99461	0.99477	0.99492	0.99506	0.99520	**2.5**
2.6	0.99534	0.99547	0.99560	0.99573	0.99585	0.99598	0.99609	0.99621	0.99632	0.99643	**2.6**
2.7	0.99653	0.99664	0.99674	0.99683	0.99693	0.99702	0.99711	0.99720	0.99728	0.99736	**2.7**
2.8	0.99744	0.99752	0.99760	0.99767	0.99774	0.99781	0.99788	0.99795	0.99801	0.99807	**2.8**
2.9	0.99813	0.99819	0.99825	0.99831	0.99836	0.99841	0.99846	0.99851	0.99856	0.99861	**2.9**
3.0	0.99865	0.99869	0.99874	0.99878	0.99882	0.99886	0.99889	0.99893	0.99896	0.99900	**3.0**
3.1	0.99903	0.99906	0.99910	0.99913	0.99916	0.99918	0.99921	0.99924	0.99926	0.99929	**3.1**
3.2	0.99931	0.99934	0.99936	0.99938	0.99940	0.99942	0.99944	0.99946	0.99948	0.99950	**3.2**
3.3	0.99952	0.99953	0.99955	0.99957	0.99958	0.99960	0.99961	0.99962	0.99964	0.99965	**3.3**
3.4	0.99966	0.99968	0.99969	0.99970	0.99971	0.99972	0.99973	0.99974	0.99975	0.99976	**3.4**
3.5	0.99977	0.99978	0.99978	0.99979	0.99980	0.99981	0.99981	0.99982	0.99983	0.99983	**3.5**
3.6	0.99984	0.99985	0.99985	0.99986	0.99986	0.99987	0.99987	0.99988	0.99988	0.99989	**3.6**
3.7	0.99989	0.99990	0.99990	0.99990	0.99991	0.99991	0.99992	0.99992	0.99992	0.99992	**3.7**
3.8	0.99993	0.99993	0.99993	0.99994	0.99994	0.99994	0.99994	0.99995	0.99995	0.99995	**3.8**
3.9	0.99995	0.99995	0.99996	0.99996	0.99996	0.99996	0.99996	0.99996	0.99997	0.99997	**3.9**

Percentage points of the normal distribution

The table gives the values of z satisfying $P(Z \leq z) = p$, where Z is the normally distributed random variable with mean = 0 and variance = 1.

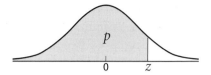

p	0.00	0.01	0.02	0.03	0.04	0.05	0.06	0.07	0.08	0.09	p
0.5	0.0000	0.0251	0.0502	0.0753	0.1004	0.1257	0.1510	0.1764	0.2019	0.2275	0.5
0.6	0.2533	0.2793	0.3055	0.3319	0.3585	0.3853	0.4125	0.4399	0.4677	0.4958	0.6
0.7	0.5244	0.5534	0.5828	0.6128	0.6433	0.6745	0.7063	0.7388	0.7722	0.8064	0.7
0.8	0.8416	0.8779	0.9154	0.9542	0.9945	1.0364	1.0803	1.1264	1.1750	1.2265	0.8
0.9	1.2816	1.3408	1.4051	1.4758	1.5548	1.6449	1.7507	1.8808	2.0537	2.3263	0.9

p	0.000	0.001	0.002	0.003	0.004	0.005	0.006	0.007	0.008	0.009	p
0.95	1.6449	1.6546	1.6646	1.6747	1.6849	1.6954	1.7060	1.7169	1.7279	1.7392	0.95
0.96	1.7507	1.7624	1.7744	1.7866	1.7991	1.8119	1.8250	1.8384	1.8522	1.8663	0.96
0.97	1.8808	1.8957	1.9110	1.9268	1.9431	1.9600	1.9774	1.9954	2.0141	2.0335	0.97
0.98	2.0537	2.0749	2.0969	2.1201	2.1444	2.1701	2.1973	2.2262	2.2571	2.2904	0.98
0.99	2.3263	2.3656	2.4089	2.4573	2.5121	2.5758	2.6521	2.7478	2.8782	3.0902	0.99

Percentage points of the Student's *t*-distribution

The table gives the values of x satisfying $P(X \leq x) = p$, where X is a random variable having the Student's *t*-distribution with v degrees of freedom.

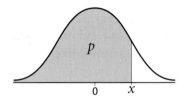

p	0.9	0.95	0.975	0.99	0.995
v					
1	3.078	6.314	12.706	31.821	63.657
2	1.886	2.920	4.303	6.965	9.925
3	1.638	2.353	3.182	4.541	5.841
4	1.533	2.132	2.776	3.747	4.604
5	1.476	2.015	2.571	3.365	4.032
6	1.440	1.943	2.447	3.143	3.707
7	1.415	1.895	2.365	2.998	3.499
8	1.397	1.860	2.306	2.896	3.355
9	1.383	1.833	2.262	2.821	3.250
10	1.372	1.812	2.228	2.764	3.169
11	1.363	1.796	2.201	2.718	3.106
12	1.356	1.782	2.179	2.681	3.055
13	1.350	1.771	2.160	2.650	3.012
14	1.345	1.761	2.145	2.624	2.977
15	1.341	1.753	2.131	2.602	2.947
16	1.337	1.746	2.121	2.583	2.921
17	1.333	1.740	2.110	2.567	2.898
18	1.330	1.734	2.101	2.552	2.878
19	1.328	1.729	2.093	2.539	2.861
20	1.325	1.725	2.086	2.528	2.845
21	1.323	1.721	2.080	2.518	2.831
22	1.321	1.717	2.074	2.508	2.819
23	1.319	1.714	2.069	2.500	2.807
24	1.318	1.711	2.064	2.492	2.797
25	1.316	1.708	2.060	2.485	2.787
26	1.315	1.706	2.056	2.479	2.779
27	1.314	1.703	2.052	2.473	2.771
28	1.313	1.701	2.048	2.467	2.763

p	0.9	0.95	0.975	0.99	0.995
v					
29	1.311	1.699	2.045	2.462	2.756
30	1.310	1.697	2.042	2.457	2.750
31	1.309	1.696	2.040	2.453	2.744
32	1.309	1.694	2.037	2.449	2.738
33	1.308	1.692	2.035	2.445	2.733
34	1.307	1.691	2.032	2.441	2.728
35	1.306	1.690	2.030	2.438	2.724
36	1.306	1.688	2.028	2.434	2.719
37	1.305	1.687	2.026	2.431	2.715
38	1.304	1.686	2.024	2.429	2.712
39	1.304	1.685	2.023	2.426	2.708
40	1.303	1.684	2.021	2.423	2.704
45	1.301	1.679	2.014	2.412	2.690
50	1.299	1.676	2.009	2.403	2.678
55	1.297	1.673	2.004	2.396	2.668
60	1.296	1.671	2.000	2.390	2.660
65	1.295	1.669	1.997	2.385	2.654
70	1.294	1.667	1.994	2.381	2.648
75	1.293	1.665	1.992	2.377	2.643
80	1.292	1.664	1.990	2.374	2.639
85	1.292	1.663	1.998	2.371	2.635
90	1.291	1.662	1.987	2.368	2.632
95	1.291	1.661	1.985	2.366	2.629
100	1.290	1.660	1.984	2.364	2.626
125	1.288	1.657	1.979	2.357	2.616
150	1.287	1.655	1.976	2.351	2.609
200	1.286	1.653	1.972	2.345	2.601
∞	1.282	1.645	1.960	2.326	2.576

Percentage points of the χ^2-distribution

The table gives the values of x satisfying $P(X \le x) = p$, where X is a random variable having the χ^2 distribution with v degrees of freedom.

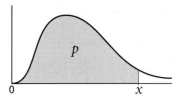

p	0.005	0.01	0.025	0.05	0.1	0.9	0.95	0.975	0.99	0.995	p
v											v
1	0.00004	0.0002	0.001	0.004	0.016	2.706	3.841	5.024	6.635	7.879	1
2	0.010	0.020	0.051	0.103	0.211	4.605	5.991	7.378	9.210	10.597	2
3	0.072	0.115	0.216	0.352	0.584	6.251	7.815	9.348	11.345	12.838	3
4	0.207	0.297	0.484	0.711	1.064	7.779	9.488	11.143	13.277	14.860	4
5	0.412	0.554	0.831	1.145	1.610	9.236	11.070	12.833	15.086	16.750	5
6	0.676	0.872	1.237	1.635	2.204	10.645	12.592	14.449	16.812	18.548	6
7	0.989	1.239	1.690	2.167	2.833	12.017	14.067	16.013	18.475	20.278	7
8	1.344	1.646	2.180	2.733	3.490	13.362	15.507	17.535	20.090	21.955	8
9	1.735	2.088	2.700	3.325	4.168	14.684	16.919	19.023	21.666	23.589	9
10	2.156	2.558	3.247	3.940	4.865	15.987	18.307	20.483	23.209	25.188	10
11	2.603	3.053	3.816	4.575	5.578	17.275	19.675	21.920	24.725	26.757	11
12	3.074	3.571	4.404	5.226	6.304	18.549	21.026	23.337	26.217	28.300	12
13	3.565	4.107	5.009	5.892	7.042	19.812	22.362	24.736	27.688	29.819	13
14	4.075	4.660	5.629	6.571	7.790	21.064	23.685	26.119	29.141	31.319	14
15	4.601	5.229	6.262	7.261	8.547	22.307	24.996	27.488	30.578	32.801	15
16	5.142	5.812	6.908	7.962	9.312	23.542	26.296	28.845	32.000	34.267	16
17	5.697	6.408	7.564	8.672	10.085	24.769	27.587	30.191	33.409	35.718	17
18	6.265	7.015	8.231	9.390	10.865	25.989	28.869	31.526	34.805	37.156	18
19	6.844	7.633	8.907	10.117	11.651	27.204	30.144	32.852	36.191	38.582	19
20	7.434	8.260	9.591	10.851	12.443	28.412	31.410	34.170	37.566	39.997	20
21	8.034	8.897	10.283	11.591	13.240	29.615	32.671	35.479	38.932	41.401	21
22	8.643	9.542	10.982	12.338	14.041	30.813	33.924	36.781	40.289	42.796	22
23	9.260	10.196	11.689	13.091	14.848	32.007	35.172	38.076	41.638	44.181	23
24	9.886	10.856	12.401	13.848	15.659	33.196	36.415	39.364	42.980	45.559	24
25	10.520	11.524	13.120	14.611	16.473	34.382	37.652	40.646	44.314	46.928	25
26	11.160	12.198	13.844	15.379	17.292	35.563	38.885	41.923	45.642	48.290	26
27	11.808	12.879	14.573	16.151	18.114	36.741	40.113	43.195	46.963	49.645	27
28	12.461	13.565	15.308	16.928	18.939	37.916	41.337	44.461	48.278	50.993	28
29	13.121	14.256	16.047	17.708	19.768	39.087	42.557	45.722	49.588	52.336	29
30	13.787	14.953	16.791	18.493	20.599	40.256	43.773	46.979	50.892	53.672	30
31	14.458	15.655	17.539	19.281	21.434	41.422	44.985	48.232	52.191	55.003	31
32	15.134	16.362	18.291	20.072	22.271	42.585	46.194	49.480	53.486	56.328	32
33	15.815	17.074	19.047	20.867	23.110	43.745	47.400	50.725	54.776	57.648	33
34	16.501	17.789	19.806	21.664	23.952	44.903	48.602	51.996	56.061	58.964	34
35	17.192	18.509	20.569	22.465	24.797	46.059	49.802	53.203	57.342	60.275	35
36	17.887	19.223	21.336	23.269	25.643	47.212	50.998	54.437	58.619	61.581	36
37	18.586	19.960	22.106	24.075	26.492	48.363	52.192	55.668	59.892	62.883	37
38	19.289	20.691	22.878	24.884	27.343	49.513	53.384	56.896	61.162	64.181	38
39	19.996	21.426	23.654	25.695	28.196	50.660	54.572	58.120	62.428	65.476	39
40	20.707	22.164	24.433	26.509	29.051	51.805	55.758	59.342	63.691	66.766	40
45	24.311	25.901	28.366	30.612	33.350	57.505	61.656	65.410	69.957	73.166	45
50	27.991	29.707	32.357	34.764	37.689	63.167	67.505	71.420	76.154	79.490	50
55	31.735	33.570	36.398	38.958	42.060	68.796	73.311	77.380	82.292	85.749	55
60	35.534	37.485	40.482	43.188	46.459	74.397	79.082	83.298	88.379	91.952	60
65	39.383	41.444	44.603	47.450	50.883	79.973	84.821	89.177	94.422	98.105	65
70	43.275	45.442	48.758	51.739	55.329	85.527	90.531	95.023	100.425	104.215	70
75	47.206	49.475	52.942	56.054	59.795	91.061	96.217	100.839	106.393	110.286	75
80	51.172	53.540	57.153	60.391	64.278	96.578	101.879	106.629	112.329	116.321	80
85	55.170	57.634	61.389	64.749	68.777	102.079	107.522	112.393	118.236	122.325	85
90	59.196	61.754	65.647	69.126	73.291	107.565	113.145	118.136	124.116	128.299	90
95	63.250	65.898	69.925	73.520	77.818	113.038	118.752	123.858	129.973	134.247	95
100	67.328	70.065	74.222	77.929	82.358	118.498	124.342	129.561	135.807	140.169	100

Answers

1 Discrete random variables

A Probability distribution (p 6)

A1 $\sum P(X = x) = 1$

A2

x	1	2	3
$P(X = x)$	$\frac{1}{2}$	$\frac{1}{3}$	$\frac{1}{6}$

A3

y	0	1	2
$P(Y = y)$	$\frac{1}{4}$	$\frac{23}{36}$	$\frac{1}{9}$

A4 $\frac{3}{18}, \frac{4}{18}, \frac{5}{18}, \frac{6}{18}$; sum $= 1$

A5 Since $\sum P(X = x) = \frac{21}{20}$ this cannot be the probability function of a discrete random variable.

A6 This cannot be the probability function of a discrete random variable since $P(X = 5)$ is negative.

Exercise A (p 8)

1

x	1	2	3	4	5
$P(X = x)$	$\frac{1}{15}$	$\frac{2}{15}$	$\frac{1}{5}$	$\frac{4}{15}$	$\frac{1}{3}$

$\frac{1}{15} + \frac{2}{15} + \frac{1}{5} + \frac{4}{15} + \frac{1}{3} = \frac{15}{15} = 1$

2

x	1	2	3	4
$P(X = x)$	$\frac{1}{5}$	$\frac{3}{10}$	$\frac{3}{10}$	$\frac{1}{5}$

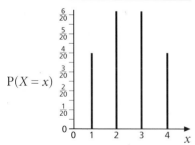

3 (a)

x	1	2	3	4
$P(X = x)$	k	$4k$	$9k$	$16k$

(b) $k + 4k + 9k + 16k = 30k = 1$ so $k = \frac{1}{30}$

(c) $P(X \geq 3) = \frac{9}{30} + \frac{16}{30} = \frac{25}{30} = \frac{5}{6}$

4

x	1	2	3	4
$P(X = x)$	$3k$	$2k$	k	k

$3k + 2k + k + k = 7k = 1$ so $k = \frac{1}{7}$

B Mean or expected value (p 9)

B1 See subsequent work.

B2 See subsequent work.

B3 Spinner A

Score	2	3	4	5
Probability	$\frac{1}{2}$	$\frac{1}{6}$	$\frac{1}{6}$	$\frac{1}{6}$

Mean score $= \left(2 \times \frac{1}{2}\right) + \left(3 \times \frac{1}{6}\right) + \left(4 \times \frac{1}{6}\right) + \left(5 \times \frac{1}{6}\right) = 3$

Spinner B

Score	2	3	4
Probability	$\frac{1}{4}$	$\frac{1}{4}$	$\frac{1}{2}$

Mean score $= \left(2 \times \frac{1}{4}\right) + \left(3 \times \frac{1}{4}\right) + \left(4 \times \frac{1}{2}\right) = 3\frac{1}{4}$

Spinner D

Score	2	3	4
Probability	$\frac{1}{5}$	$\frac{2}{5}$	$\frac{2}{5}$

Mean score $= \left(2 \times \frac{1}{5}\right) + \left(3 \times \frac{2}{5}\right) + \left(4 \times \frac{2}{5}\right) = 3\frac{1}{5}$

Spinner B is better than spinner A $\left(3\frac{1}{4} > 3\right)$.

Spinner C is better than spinner D $\left(3\frac{1}{3} > 3\frac{1}{5}\right)$.

B4 1.15

B5 0.9; you will lose an average of 10p per game.

B6 (a)

y	0	1	10
$P(Y = y)$	0.75	0.2	0.05

(b) 0.7   (c) Better

B7 (a)

x	-10	5	20
$P(X = x)$	$\frac{5}{9}$	$\frac{5}{18}$	$\frac{1}{6}$

(b) $-\frac{5}{6}$; on average, Carl loses $\frac{5}{6}$p for every game they play.

B8 (a)

y	-10	20	50
$P(Y = y)$	$\frac{3}{4}$	$\frac{1}{8}$	$\frac{1}{8}$

(b) $\frac{5}{4} = 1.25$; on average, Carl wins 1.25p for every game they play.

B9 $a + 2b = 1.5$ and $a + b = 0.85$ so $a = 0.2$ and $b = 0.65$

Exercise B (p 11)

1 (a) 0.42   **(b)** 2.04

2 (a) $\frac{1}{50}$ (b) 2

3 (a) 0.1   (b) 0.2

4 $\alpha = 0.1$, $\beta = 0.3$

5 4.5

C Expectation of a function of a discrete random variable (p 12)

C1 (a) 2.5   (b) 5   (c) $E(Y) = 2E(X)$

C2 (a)

Value of W	4	5	6	7
Probability	$\frac{1}{4}$	$\frac{1}{4}$	$\frac{1}{4}$	$\frac{1}{4}$

(b) 5.5

(c) $E(W) = E(X) + 3$

C3 (a)

Value of V	5	7	9	11
Probability	$\frac{1}{4}$	$\frac{1}{4}$	$\frac{1}{4}$	$\frac{1}{4}$

(b) 8

(c) $E(V) = 2E(X) + 3$

C4 (a) The student's idea

(b)

Value of U	9	13	17	21
Probability	$\frac{1}{4}$	$\frac{1}{4}$	$\frac{1}{4}$	$\frac{1}{4}$

$E(U) = \left(9 \times \frac{1}{4}\right) + \left(13 \times \frac{1}{4}\right) + \left(17 \times \frac{1}{4}\right) + \left(21 \times \frac{1}{4}\right)$
$= 15$

C5 $E(aX + b) = aE(X) + b$

C6 (a) 12.5   (b) 10.5   (c) -7.5
(d) -6.5 (e) 5

C7 (a) $E(Y) = (12 \times 0.1) + (6 \times 0.3) + (4 \times 0.4) + (3 \times 0.2) = 5.2$

(b) $\frac{12}{E(X)} = \frac{12}{2.7} = 4.444$

but $E(Y) = 5.2$ so $\frac{12}{E(X)} \neq E(Y)$

C8 (a) $E(X^2) = \left(1 \times \frac{1}{6}\right) + \left(4 \times \frac{1}{6}\right) + \left(9 \times \frac{1}{6}\right) + \left(16 \times \frac{1}{6}\right)$
$+ \left(25 \times \frac{1}{6}\right) + \left(36 \times \frac{1}{6}\right) = \frac{91}{6} = 15\frac{1}{6}$

(b) $E(X) = 3\frac{1}{2}$
$[E(X)]^2 = \left(3\frac{1}{2}\right)^2 = 12\frac{1}{4}$
but $E(X^2) = 15\frac{1}{6}$ so $E(X^2) \neq [E(X)]^2$

C9 (a)

y^2	1	4	9	16
$P(Y^2 = y^2)$	0.1	0.3	0.4	0.2

$E(Y^2) = (1 \times 0.1) + (4 \times 0.3) + (9 \times 0.4)$
$+ (16 \times 0.2) = 8.1$

(b) $E(Y) = 2.7$
$[E(Y)]^2 = (2.7)^2 = 7.29$
but $E(Y^2) = 8.1$ so $E(Y^2) \neq [E(Y)]^2$

Exercise C (p 15)

1 (a) 12.75   (b) 16.75   (c) -8.5 (d) -1.5

2 (a) 2.3   (b) 8.9   (c) 3.4

3 (a) $\frac{1}{20}$ (b) 3.6   (c) 2.4   (d) 17

4 (a) 2.05

(b) $(1 \times 0.25) + (4 \times 0.3) + (9 \times 0.2) + (16 \times 0.15)$
$= 5.65$

(c) $(1 \times 0.25) + (8 \times 0.3) + (27 \times 0.2) + (64 \times 0.15)$
$= 17.65$

5 (a) 5   (b) 9

6

$\frac{24}{x+1}$	24	12	8	6
Probability	0.05	0.55	0.25	0.15

$E\left(\dfrac{24}{X+1}\right) = 10.7$

7

$\frac{60}{t}$	60	30	20	15	12
Probability	$\frac{1}{55}$	$\frac{4}{55}$	$\frac{9}{55}$	$\frac{16}{55}$	$\frac{25}{55}$

$E\left(\dfrac{60}{T}\right) = \dfrac{900}{55} = 16\frac{4}{11}$

D Variance and standard deviation (p 16)

D1 (a) $E(X) = E(Y) = 1.9$

(b) The distribution for game A is more spread out than for game B.

D2 $\text{Var}(X) = (0 - 1.9)^2 \times 0.15 + (1 - 1.9)^2 \times 0.25$
$+ (2 - 1.9)^2 \times 0.25 + (3 - 1.9)^2 \times 0.25$
$+ (4 - 1.9)^2 \times 0.1$
$= 3.61 \times 0.15 + 0.81 \times 0.25 + 0.01 \times 0.25$
$+ 1.21 \times 0.25 + 4.41 \times 0.1$
$= 1.49$

D3 (a) 4.4

(b) $E(Y^2) - [E(Y)]^2 = 4.4 - 1.9^2 = 0.79$

(c) Game A has the greater variance. The marks are more spread out on the graph.

Exercise D (p 18)

1 (a) 2.04   **(b)** 0.8184

2 (a) 3.05   **(b)** 1.0475

3 Mean = 2.375, variance = 1.984 38

4 $E(X) = 4.5$, $Var(X) = 1.75$

5 (a) $a + b = 0.5$ and $a + 3b = 0.6$ so $a = 0.45$ and $b = 0.05$

  (b) 0.66

E Variance of a function of a discrete random variable (p 18)

E1 (a) 0.81

  (b) (i) 3.4

    (ii) $E(Y^2) = 14.8$, $Var(Y) = 3.24$

  (c) No; $Var(Y) = 4\,Var(X)$

E2 (a) 0.65

  (b) The student's idea

  (c)

y	2	5	8	11
$P(Y = y)$	0.05	0.55	0.25	0.15

    $Var(Y) = 5.85$

  (d) $Var(Y) = 9\,Var(X)$

E3 (a) 0.81

  (b) (i) 12.96   **(ii)** 7.29

E4 (a)

y	12	6	4	3
$P(Y = y)$	0.2	0.4	0.3	0.1

  (b) $E(Y) = 6.3$, $E(Y^2) = 48.9$

  (c) $Var(Y) = 48.9 - 6.3^2 = 9.21$

  (d) $\dfrac{12}{Var(X)} = \dfrac{12}{0.81} = 14.81$ (to 2 d.p.)

    but $Var\left(\dfrac{12}{X}\right) = 9.21$ so $\dfrac{12}{Var(X)} \neq Var\left(\dfrac{12}{X}\right)$

Exercise E (p 20)

1 (a) 7.5   **(b)** 8   **(c)** 5   **(d)** 11.25

2 (a) 6   **(b)** 2.88   **(c)** 3.5   **(d)** 0.02

3 (a) $\frac{1}{20}$ **(b)** 2.5   **(c)** 1.75   **(d)** 7

4 (a) 11π **(b)** $74.8\pi^2$ **(c)** $\sqrt{74.8}\,\pi = 8.65\pi$

5 (a) 0.89   **(b)** 26.01   **(c)** 26.76

6 $a = 3$, $b = 6$

7 (a) $Var(T) = E(T^2) - [E(T)]^2$
             $= 35 - 5^2$
             $= 10$

  (b) $Var(T^2) = E(T^4) - [E(T^2)]^2$
                $= 1250 - 35^2$
                $= 25$

8 (a) $E(V^2) = Var(V) + [E(V)]^2$
            $= 4.25 + 2.5^2$
            $= 10.5$

  (b) $E(V^2) - E(V) = 8$

9 (a) (i) 3.15   **(ii)** 11.35   **(iii)** 1.4275

  (b) $4W + 20$

  (c) Mean = 32.6, variance = 22.84

  (d) Area = $W(W + 10) = W^2 + 10W$

  (e) 42.85

10 (a) Mean = 25, variance = 120

  (b) (i)

$\dfrac{60}{R}$	60	30	20	15	12
Probability	0.1	0.2	0.4	0.2	0.1

    (ii) $(60 \times 0.1) + (30 \times 0.2) + (20 \times 0.4)$
           $+ (15 \times 0.2) + (12 \times 0.1)$
           $= 6 + 6 + 8 + 3 + 1.2$
           $= 24.2$

    (iii) $759.4 - 24.2^2 = 173.76$

Mixed questions (p 22)

1 (a) 3.1   **(b)** 1.29   **(c)** 11.3   **(d)** 5.16

2 (a) $\frac{1}{50}$ **(b)** 5.2   **(c)** 1.08   **(d)** 13.6   **(e)** 9.72

3 (a)

x	1	2	3	4	5	6
$P(X = x)$	0.09	0.09	0.09	0.09	0.09	0.55

  (b) $E(X) = 4.65$, $Var(X) = 3.1275$

4 (a) $\alpha = 0.05$, $\beta = 0.45$ **(b)** 3.85

  (c) 1.1275   **(d)** 2.3   **(e)** 4.51

5 (a) $\alpha = 0.15$, $\beta = 0.25$ **(b)** 1.8

  (c) 1.79   **(d)** 5.1   **(e)** 1.79

6 (a) $20b + 0.45$

(b) $a = 0.8225$, $b = 0.0275$

(c) £0.35

7 (a) (i) 1.8   (ii) 12.66   (iii) 1.75   (iv) 24.3875

(b) Machine A, as the value of $E(X)$ is higher

(c) Machine A: 20p; machine B: 25p

(d) There is a bigger chance of getting £20 or nothing on machine B.

8 (a) Mean = 40, variance = 900

(b) (i) $E(T^2) = \text{Var}(T) + [E(T)]^2 = 25 + 5^2 = 50$

(ii) 150

9 (a) Mean = 4π, variance = $4\pi^2$

(b) 5π

Test yourself (p 24)

1 (a) $E(V) = (1 \times 0.15) + (2 \times 0.45) + (3 \times 0.20)$
$+ (4 \times 0.15) + (5 \times 0.05)$
$= 0.15 + 0.90 + 0.60 + 0.60 + 0.25$
$= 2.5$

$E(V^2) = (1 \times 0.15) + (4 \times 0.45) + (9 \times 0.20)$
$+ (16 \times 0.15) + (25 \times 0.05)$
$= 0.15 + 1.80 + 1.80 + 2.40 + 1.25$
$= 7.4$

$\text{Var}(V) = E(V^2) - [E(V)]^2 = 7.4 - 2.5^2 = 1.15$

(b) Mean = £100, variance = £1035

(c) £383.50

2 (a) Mean = 10, variance = 25

(b) Mean = 4.8, variance = 6.96

3 (a) (i) $E(R) = (1 \times 0.1) + (2 \times 0.2) + (3 \times 0.4)$
$+ (4 \times 0.2) + (5 \times 0.1)$
$= 0.1 + 0.4 + 1.2 + 0.8 + 0.5$
$= 3$

(ii) $E(R^2) = (1 \times 0.1) + (4 \times 0.2) + (9 \times 0.4)$
$+ (16 \times 0.2) + (25 \times 0.1)$
$= 0.1 + 0.8 + 3.6 + 3.2 + 2.5$
$= 10.2$

$\text{Var}(R) = E(R^2) - [E(R)]^2 = 10.2 - 3^2 = 1.2$

(b) $E(P) = 13$, $\text{Var}(P) = 10.8$

(c) (i) $C = 196 - 4R$

(ii) Mean = 184, variance = 19.2

2 Poisson distribution

A The Poisson model (p 25)

Answers are given to three decimal places

A1

x	0	1	2
$P(X = x)$ by observation	0.17	0.30	0.27
$P(X = x) = e^{-\lambda}\dfrac{\lambda^x}{x!}$	0.172	0.303	0.266

3	4	5	6	≥ 7
0.16	0.07	0.02	0.01	0
0.156	0.069	0.024	0.007	0.002

Data from the Poisson model is the same as the observed data when rounded to 2 d.p.

A2 (a) 0.161   (b) 0.161   (c) 0.138

A3 (a) 0.050   (b) 0.149   (c) 0.224

(d) 0.224   (e) 0.353

Exercise A (p 28)

Answers are given to three decimal places

1 (a) 0.223   (b) 0.251   (c) 0.934   (d) 0.019

2 (a) 0.015   (b) 0.185   (c) 0.605

3 (a) 0.033   (b) 0.660

4 (a) 0.449   (b) 0.359   (c) 0.192

5 (a) 0.082   (b) 0.214   (c) 0.042

6 (a) 0.301   (b) 0.578   (c) 0.121

7 (a) (i) 0.224   (ii) 0.224

(b) (i) 0.175   (ii) 0.175

(c) $P(X = x) = \dfrac{e^{-\lambda}\lambda^x}{x!}$ so $P(X = \lambda) = \dfrac{e^{-\lambda}\lambda^\lambda}{\lambda!}$

$= \dfrac{e^{-\lambda}\lambda^{\lambda-1}\lambda}{\lambda(\lambda-1)!} = \dfrac{e^{-\lambda}\lambda^{\lambda-1}}{(\lambda-1)!} = P(X = \lambda - 1)$

B The Poisson table (p 29)

B1 (a) 0.8335

(b) $P(X \leq 2) - P(X \leq 1) = 0.2417$

(c) $1 - P(X \leq 2) = 0.1665$

(d) $1 - P(X \leq 1) = 0.4082$

(e) $P(X \leq 3) - P(X \leq 0) = 0.6997$

B2 (a) $P(Y \le 3) = 0.9212$

(b) $1 - P(Y \le 2) = 0.2166$

(c) $1 - P(Y \le 0) = 0.7981$

(d) $P(Y \le 5) - P(Y \le 4) = 0.0177$

(e) $P(Y \le 5) - P(Y \le 1) = 0.4691$

Exercise B (p 30)

1 (a) 0.8946   **(b)** 0.2226   **(c)** 0.6201

(d) 0.0446   **(e)** 0.5147

2 (a) 0.9659   **(b)** 0.0283   **(c)** 0.0058

3 (a) 0.0111   **(b)** 0.1687   **(c)** 0.2971

4 (a) 0.5488   **(b)** 0.0034

5 (a) 0.1140   **(b)** 0.1054

6 (a) 0.3690   **(b)** 0.3272

7 (a) 0.0907   **(b)** 0.2177   **(c)** 0.2213

C Mean, variance and standard deviation

Exercise C (p 31)

1 (a) 0.4066   **(b)** 0.0003   **(c)** 0.9

2 (a) Mean = 6.5, variance = 6.5,
standard deviation = 2.550 (to 3 d.p.)

(b) Values within 1 s.d. from the mean are
4, 5, 6, 7, 8, 9. Probability = 0.7656

3 (a) Mean = 2.3, variance = 3.13

(b) For a Poisson distribution, the mean should
equal the variance.

D Independent Poisson distributions

Exercise D (p 33)

Answers are given to four decimal places

1 (a) 0.9212   **(b)** 0.0602

(c) $X + Y \sim Po(4)$, 0.8893

(d) $1 - P(X + Y \le 6) = 0.1107$

2 (a) 0.0116

(b) $C + V \sim Po(3.2)$, $P(C + V > 6) = 1 - 0.9554$
= 0.0446

3 (a) 0.2231

(b) 0.7769

(c) 0.3347

(d) The total number of errors, $E \sim Po(4.5)$,
$P(E > 5) = 0.2971$

(e) $(0.7769)^3 = 0.4689$

4 The total number of errors $\sim Po(3.1)$
The probability of more than 2 errors = 0.5988

5 (a) $1 - 0.2424 = 0.7576$

(b) $(0.2381)^3 = 0.0135$

6 (a) (i) 0.0408   **(ii)** 0.9592

(b) (i) 0.99996   **(ii)** $(0.9592)^4 = 0.8465$

7 The calls do not arrive at random as they can only
be received when the telephone is not in use.

8 (a) (i) 0.6973

(ii) $(0.6973)^3 = 0.3390$

(b) Let X be the number of vehicles arriving in a
10-minute period.
$X \sim Po(7.2)$
$$P(X = 0) = \frac{e^{-7.2}7.2^0}{0!} = 0.0007$$

Mixed questions (p 35)

1 (a) $X + Y \sim Po(6)$ **(b)** 6

2 (a) 0.1353   **(b)** 0.9817   **(c)** 0.1170

3 (a) (i) P(arrivals between 9 and 10 a.m. ≤ 3)
= 0.4335

(ii) P(arrivals between 9 and 10 a.m. ≤ 3)
$\times$P(arrivals between 10 and 11 a.m. ≤ 3)
= $0.4335^2 = 0.1879$

(iii) P(arrivals between 9 and 10 a.m. = 4)
$\times$P(arrivals between 10 and 11 a.m. ≤ 2)
= $0.1953 \times 0.2381 = 0.0465$

(b) To cases (ii) and (iii) above, you have to add
these:
P(arrivals between 9 and 10 a.m. = 5)
$\times$P(arrivals between 10 and 11 a.m. ≤ 1)
and
P(arrivals between 9 and 10 a.m. = 6)
$\times$P(arrivals between 10 and 11 a.m. = 0)
Overall probability = 0.2507

4 (a) (i) Poisson with mean 0.4

(ii) Poisson with mean 0.6

(iii) Poisson with mean 0.8

(b) 0.1813

(c) 0.3297

(d) 0.1484

(e) (i) 0.1215   **(ii)** 0.0995

(f) λt

(g) Let W = waiting time

$P(t < W < t + h) = P(W < t + h) - P(W < t)$

$P(W < t) = P(\text{number of emissions in time } t \geq 0)$
$\qquad = 1 - e^{-\lambda t}$

$P(W < t + h)$
$= P(\text{number of emissions in time } t + h \geq 0)$
$= 1 - e^{-\lambda(t + h)}$

So $P(t < W < t + h) = 1 - e^{-\lambda(t + h)} - (1 - e^{-\lambda t})$
$\qquad\qquad\qquad = e^{-\lambda t} - e^{-\lambda(t + h)}$
$\qquad\qquad\qquad = e^{-\lambda t}(1 - e^{-\lambda h})$

Test yourself (p 36)

1 (a) 0.1108   **(b)** 0.2438   **(c)** 0.6454

2 (a) 0.6728   **(b)** 0.1463

3 (a) 0.4628   **(b)** 0.1607

4 (a) 0.8335   **(b)** 0.0394   **(c)** 0.4082

5 (a) (i) 0.9526   **(ii)** 0.5507   **(iii)** 0.3595

(b) (i) Poisson distribution with mean 4

(ii) 0.3712

(iii) 0.0506

6 (a) (i) 0.8335   **(ii)** 0.3081

(b) 0.7787

(c) 0.0909

(d) Either of the following: the mean may vary according to the day of the week; letters may not be independent but may arrive in groups.

3 Continuous random variables

A Probability density function (p 38)

A1 Area $= \int_0^1 2(1 - x)\,dx = \left[2x - x^2\right]_0^1 = 1$

A2 (a) $f(x)$

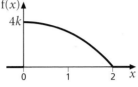

(b) Area $= \int_0^2 k(4 - x^2)\,dx = k\left[4x - \tfrac{1}{3}x^3\right]_0^2 = k(8 - \tfrac{8}{3})$
$\qquad = \dfrac{16k}{3}$

(c) $\dfrac{16k}{3} = 1 \ \Rightarrow \ k = \tfrac{3}{16}$

A3 $\int_0^{0.5} 2(1 - x)\,dx = 0.75$

A4 $\int_0^1 \tfrac{3}{16}(4 - x^2)\,dx = \tfrac{3}{16}\left[4x - \tfrac{1}{3}x^3\right]_0^1 = \tfrac{3}{16}\left(4 - \tfrac{1}{3}\right) = \tfrac{11}{16}$

A5 (a) $\int_0^1 6x(1 - x)\,dx = \left[3x^2 - 2x^3\right]_0^1 = 3 - 2 = 1$

(b) $\int_0^{0.4} 6x(1 - x)\,dx = 0.352$

(c) $\int_{0.4}^{0.6} 6x(1 - x)\,dx = 0.296$

A6 (a) $f(x)$

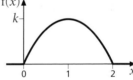

(b) Area $= \int_0^2 kx(2 - x)\,dx = k\left[x^2 - \tfrac{1}{3}x^3\right]_0^2 = k(4 - \tfrac{8}{3})$
$\qquad = \dfrac{4k}{3}$

(c) $\dfrac{4k}{3} = 1 \ \Rightarrow \ k = \tfrac{3}{4}$

(d) $P(X \leq 1.5) = P(X \leq 0) + P(0 \leq X \leq 1.5)$
As $P(X \leq 0) = 0$, $P(X \leq 1.5) = P(0 \leq X \leq 1.5)$
$\int_0^{1.5} \tfrac{3}{4}x(2 - x)\,dx = \tfrac{27}{32} = 0.84375$

(e) $\tfrac{5}{32}$ or 0.15625

A7 (a) $\int_0^1 \tfrac{3}{4}x^2\,dx = \left[\tfrac{1}{4}x^3\right]_0^1 = \tfrac{1}{4}$

$\int_1^3 \tfrac{3}{8}(3 - x)\,dx = \tfrac{3}{8}\left[3x - \tfrac{1}{2}x^2\right]_1^3$
$= \tfrac{3}{8}(9 - \tfrac{9}{2}) - \tfrac{3}{8}(3 - \tfrac{1}{2}) = \tfrac{3}{4}$

$\int_0^1 \tfrac{3}{4}x^2\,dx + \int_1^2 \tfrac{3}{8}(3 - x)\,dx = \tfrac{1}{4} + \tfrac{3}{4} = 1$

(b) $\int_{0.5}^{1}\frac{3}{4}x^2\,dx + \int_{1}^{2}\frac{3}{8}(3-x)\,dx = \frac{7}{32} + \frac{9}{16} = \frac{25}{32}$

Exercise A (p 42)

1 (a) f(x)

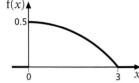

(b) $\int_{0}^{3}\frac{1}{18}(9-x^2)\,dx = \frac{1}{18}\left[9x - \frac{1}{3}x^3\right]_{0}^{3} = \frac{1}{18}(27-9) = 1$

(c) (i) $\frac{13}{27}$ **(ii)** $\frac{10}{27}$ **(iii)** $\frac{4}{27}$

2 (a) f(x)

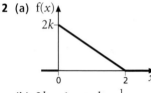

(b) $2k = 1 \Rightarrow k = \frac{1}{2}$

(c) $\frac{1}{4}$

3 (a) f(x)

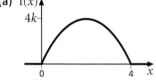

(b) $\frac{32k}{3} = 1 \Rightarrow k = \frac{3}{32}$

(c) $\frac{27}{32}$

4 (a) f(s)

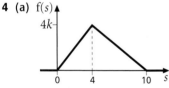

(b) Area $= \int_{0}^{4} ks\,ds + \int_{4}^{10}\frac{2}{3}k(10-s)\,ds$

$= k\left[\frac{1}{2}s^2\right]_{0}^{4} + \frac{2}{3}k\left[10s - \frac{1}{2}s^2\right]_{4}^{10}$

$= 8k + \frac{100}{3}k - \frac{64}{3}k = 8k + 12k = 20k$

(c) $20k = 1 \Rightarrow k = \frac{1}{20}$

(d) $\frac{43}{120}$

5 (a) $\frac{3}{4}$ **(b)** $\frac{5}{16}$

6 (a) f(t)

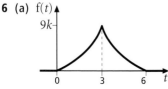

(b) $\int_{0}^{3} kt^2\,dt + \int_{3}^{6} k(6-t)^2\,dt = k\left[\frac{1}{3}t^3\right]_{0}^{3} + k\left[-\frac{1}{3}(6-t)^3\right]_{3}^{6}$

$= 9k + k(0+9) = 18k$

$18k = 1 \Rightarrow k = \frac{1}{18}$

(c) $\frac{5}{6}$

B Distribution function (p 43)

B1 $\int_{0}^{a}\frac{3}{4}x(2-x)\,dx = \frac{3}{4}\left[x^2 - \frac{1}{3}x^3\right]_{0}^{a} = \frac{3}{4}\left(a^2 - \frac{1}{3}a^3\right)$

$= \frac{3}{4}a^2 - \frac{1}{4}a^3 = \frac{1}{4}a^2(3-a)$

B2 (a) f(x)

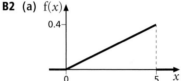

(b) $\int_{0}^{a} 0.08x\,dx = 0.04a^2$

(c) $F(X) = P(X < x) = 0.04x^2$

(d) $P(X < 2.5) = 0.04(2.5)^2 = 0.25$

B3 (a) $\int_{0}^{a} 0.003s^2\,ds = 0.001a^3$

$F(s) = P(S < s) = 0.001s^3$

(b) $0.001(8)^3 = 0.512$

B4 $f(x) = F'(x) = \frac{1}{2} - \frac{1}{8}x$

Exercise B (p 44)

1 (a) (i) $F(x) = 0.01x^2 \quad (0 \le x \le 10)$

(ii) 0.01

(b) (i) $F(x) = 0.04(10x - x^2) \quad (0 \le x \le 5)$

(ii) 0.36

(c) (i) $F(x) = 0.008x^3 \quad (0 \le x \le 5)$

(ii) 0.008

(d) (i) $F(x) = \frac{1}{16}x^2(6 - x) \quad (0 \le x \le 2)$

(ii) $\frac{5}{16}$

2 (a) (i) $P(X \ge 1) = 1 - P(X < 1) = 1 - F(1)$

$= 1 - \frac{1}{4} = \frac{3}{4}$

(ii) $f(x) = \frac{1}{2}x \quad (0 \le x \le 2)$

(b) (i) $\frac{1}{2}$

(ii) $f(x) = \frac{3}{4}x(2 - x) \quad (0 \le x \le 2)$

C Median, quartiles and percentiles (p 45)

Answers are given to three significant figures.

C1 Area $= \int_{0}^{3}\frac{1}{9}x^2\,dx = \left[\frac{1}{27}x^3\right]_{0}^{3} = 1$

C2 (a) $\int_0^m \frac{1}{9}x^2\,dx = \left[\frac{1}{27}x^3\right]_0^m = \frac{1}{27}m^3$

(b) $\frac{1}{27}m^3 = \frac{1}{2} \Rightarrow m = \sqrt[3]{13.5} = 2.38$

C3 (a) $\int_0^l \frac{1}{9}x^2\,dx = \frac{1}{27}l^3$

$\frac{1}{27}l^3 = \frac{1}{4} \Rightarrow l = \sqrt[3]{\frac{27}{4}} = 1.89$

(b) $\int_0^u \frac{1}{9}x^2\,dx = \frac{1}{27}u^3$

$\frac{1}{27}u^3 = \frac{3}{4} \Rightarrow u = \sqrt[3]{\frac{81}{4}} = 2.73$

C4 (a) $\int_0^{P_{20}} \frac{1}{9}x^2\,dx = \frac{1}{27}P_{20}^{\ 3}$

$\frac{1}{27}P_{20}^{\ 3} = 0.20 \Rightarrow P_{20} = \sqrt[3]{5.4} = 1.75$

(b) $\frac{1}{27}P_{80}^{\ 3} = 0.80 \Rightarrow P_{80} = 2.78$

C5 (a) Area $= \int_0^2 \frac{1}{5}x\,dx + \int_2^5 \frac{2}{15}(5-x)\,dx$

$= \left[\frac{1}{10}x^2\right]_0^2 + \frac{2}{15}\left[5x - \frac{1}{2}x^2\right]_2^5$

$= \frac{2}{5} + \left[\frac{5}{3} - \frac{16}{15}\right] = \frac{2}{5} + \frac{9}{15} = 1$

(b) To the right

(c) $\int_m^5 \frac{2}{15}(5-x)\,dx = \frac{2}{15}\left[5x - \frac{1}{2}x^2\right]_m^5$

$= \frac{5}{3} - \frac{2}{15}\left(5m - \frac{1}{2}m^2\right)$

$= \frac{5}{3} - \frac{2}{3}m + \frac{1}{15}m^2$

As m is the median, $\frac{5}{3} - \frac{2}{3}m + \frac{1}{15}m^2 = \frac{1}{2}$

$\Rightarrow \quad 50 - 20m + 2m^2 = 15$

$\Rightarrow \quad 2m^2 - 20m + 35 = 0$

$m = 2.26$ (the other solution, $m = 7.74$, is outside the given range)

(d) $\int_0^l \frac{1}{5}x\,dx = 0.25 \Rightarrow l = 1.58$

$\int_u^5 \frac{2}{15}(5-x)\,dx = 0.25 \Rightarrow u = 3.06$

C6 (a) $F(u) = \frac{3}{4} \Rightarrow 0.04u(10 - u) = 0.75$

$\Rightarrow 4u(10 - u) = 75$

$\Rightarrow 4u^2 - 40u + 75 = 0$

(b) $(2u - 5)(2u - 15) = 0$

$\Rightarrow u = 2.5$ ($u = 7.5$ is outside the range)

(c) $0.04p(10 - p) = 0.64 \Rightarrow p(10 - p) = 16$

$\Rightarrow p^2 - 10p + 16 = 0$

$\Rightarrow (p - 2)(p - 8) = 0$

$\Rightarrow p = 2$ ($p = 8$ is outside the range)

Exercise C (p 47)

1 (a) f(x)

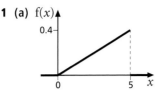

(b) 3.54 (to 3 s.f.)   **(c)** 2.5

(d) 4.47 (to 3 s.f.)

2 (a) f(t)

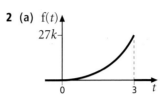

(b) $\frac{4}{81}$ **(c)** 2.52 (to 3 s.f.)

(d) 2.12 (to 3 s.f.)

3 (a) The area is triangular with base 6 units and height k units, so area $= \frac{1}{2} \times 6 \times k = 3k$
Area $= 1$, so $k = \frac{1}{3}$

(b) f(x) $= \frac{1}{12}x$

(c) The gradient is $\dfrac{-\frac{1}{3}}{2} = -\frac{1}{6}$
The equation is of the form f(x) $= -\frac{1}{6}x + c$
When $x = 6$, f(x) $= 0$, so $c = 1$

(d) (i) $\int_0^m \frac{1}{12}x\,dx = \frac{1}{2} \Rightarrow m = 3.46$

(ii) $l = 2.45$

(iii) $\int_u^6 \left(1 - \frac{1}{6}x\right)dx = \frac{1}{4} \Rightarrow u = 4.27$

4 (a) $P(U < m) = \int_0^m \frac{1}{24}(8 - u)\,du = \frac{1}{24}\left[8u - \frac{1}{2}u^2\right]_0^m$
$= \frac{1}{24}\left(8m - \frac{1}{2}m^2\right)$, which is $\frac{1}{2}$
So $8m - \frac{1}{2}m^2 = 12 \Rightarrow m^2 - 16m + 24 = 0$

(b) 1.7

5 (a) f(t)

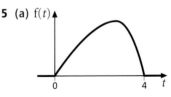

(b) $\frac{1}{64}$

(c) (i) $\int_0^m \frac{1}{64}t(16-t^2)\,dt = \int_0^m \frac{1}{64}(16t-t^3)\,dt$

$$= \frac{1}{64}\left[8t^2 - \frac{t^4}{4}\right]_0^m = \frac{1}{64}\left(8m^2 - \frac{m^4}{4}\right)$$

As $\int_0^m \frac{1}{64}t(16-t^2)\,dt = \frac{1}{2}$

then $\frac{1}{64}\left(8m^2 - \frac{m^4}{4}\right) = \frac{1}{2}$

$$\Rightarrow 8m^2 - \frac{m^4}{4} = 32 \;\Rightarrow\; m^4 - 32m^2 + 128 = 0$$

(ii) $m = 2.2$

D Mean or expected value (p 49)

D1 (a) $\frac{1}{2}\int_0^2 x^2\,dx = \frac{1}{2}\left[\frac{1}{3}x^3\right]_0^2 = \frac{4}{3}$

(b) If the graph were symmetrical about $x = 1$, then $E(X)$ would be 1. But intervals > 1 have higher probabilities than intervals < 1, so $E(X) > 1$.

D2 $E(X)\int_0^3 x\left(\frac{1}{9}x^2\right)dx = \frac{1}{9}\int_0^3 x^3\,dx = \frac{1}{36}\left[x^4\right]_0^3 = 2\frac{1}{4}$

D3 $E(X) = \frac{1}{5}\int_0^2 x^2\,dx + \frac{2}{15}\int_2^5(5x-x^2)\,dx$

$$= \frac{1}{5}\left[\frac{1}{3}x^3\right]_0^2 + \frac{2}{15}\left[\frac{5}{2}x^2 - \frac{1}{3}x^3\right]_2^5$$

$$= \frac{1}{5}\left(\frac{8}{3}\right) + \frac{2}{15}\left[\left(\frac{125}{2} - \frac{125}{3}\right) - \left(10 - \frac{8}{3}\right)\right]$$

$$= \frac{8}{15} + \frac{2}{15}\left(\frac{27}{2}\right)$$

$$= 2\frac{1}{3}$$

Exercise D (p 50)

1 $1\frac{7}{9}$

2 $\frac{7}{12}$

3 $1\frac{1}{8}$

4 (a) $\frac{1}{4}$ **(b)** $1\frac{3}{5}$

5 (a) f(x)

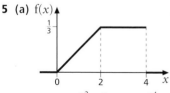

(b) $E(X) = \int_0^2 x\left(\frac{1}{6}x\right)dx + \int_2^4 x\left(\frac{1}{3}\right)dx = 2\frac{4}{9}$

6 (a) f(u)

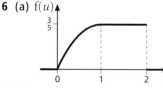

(b) $E(U) = \int_0^1 u\left(\frac{3}{5}u(2-u)\right)du + \int_1^2 u\left(\frac{3}{5}\right)du = 1\frac{3}{20}$

7 (a) f(x)

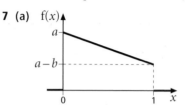

f(0) = a and f(1) = a − b

f(x) is a probability density function so
f(x) ≥ 0. Because f(1) ≥ 0, a − b ≥ 0 so a ≥ b
Also, because f(0) ≥ 0, a ≥ 0.

(b) The area under the graph forms a trapezium. The area is

$\frac{1}{2}\times 1\times(a + (a - b)) = \frac{1}{2}(2a - b) = a - \frac{1}{2}b.$
Because it is a probability density function,
$a - \frac{1}{2}b = 1$

(c) $\int_0^1 x(a - bx)\,dx = \frac{3}{8} \;\Rightarrow\; \frac{1}{2}a - \frac{1}{3}b = \frac{3}{8}$

(d) $a = \frac{7}{4},\; b = \frac{3}{2}$

E Expectation of a function of a continuous random variable (p 52)

E1 $E\left(\frac{1}{X}\right) = \int_0^3 \frac{1}{x}\left(\frac{1}{3}x^2\right)dx = \frac{1}{3}\int_0^3 x\,dx = \frac{1}{3}\left[\frac{1}{2}x^2\right]_0^3 = \frac{1}{3}\left(\frac{9}{2}\right) = \frac{3}{2}$

E2 (a) $E(X^2) = \int_0^3 x^2\left(\frac{1}{3}x^2\right)dx = \frac{1}{3}\int_0^3 x^4\,dx = \frac{1}{3}\left[\frac{1}{5}x^5\right]_0^3$

$$= \frac{1}{3}\left(\frac{243}{5}\right) = 16\frac{1}{5}$$

(b) $E(X^3) = \int_0^3 x^3\left(\frac{1}{3}x^2\right)dx = \frac{1}{3}\int_0^3 x^5\,dx = \frac{1}{3}\left[\frac{1}{6}x^6\right]_0^3$

$$= \frac{1}{3}\left(\frac{243}{2}\right) = 40\frac{1}{2}$$

E3 (a) $E(X) = \int_0^3 x\left(\frac{1}{3}x^2\right)dx = \frac{1}{3}\int_0^3 x^3\,dx = \frac{1}{3}\left[\frac{1}{4}x^4\right]_0^3$

$$= \frac{1}{3}\left(\frac{81}{4}\right) = 6\frac{3}{4}$$

(b) $E(3X + 2) = 3E(X) + 2 = 3\left(6\frac{3}{4}\right) + 2 = 22\frac{1}{4}$

(c) $E\left(\frac{1}{2}X - 1\right) = \frac{1}{2}E(X) - 1 = \frac{1}{2}\left(6\frac{3}{4}\right) - 1 = 2\frac{3}{8}$

E4 (a) $E\left(\frac{3}{X} + 1\right) = 3E\left(\frac{1}{X}\right) + 1 = 3\left(\frac{3}{2}\right) + 1 = 5\frac{1}{2}$

(b) $E(4X^2 - 3) = 4E(X^2) - 3 = 4\left(16\frac{1}{5}\right) - 3 = 61\frac{4}{5}$

(c) $E\left(20 - \frac{1}{5}X^3\right) = 20 - \frac{1}{5}E(X^3) = 20 - \frac{1}{5}\left(40\frac{1}{2}\right) = 11\frac{9}{10}$

Exercise E (p 53)

1 (a) 7.5   **(b)** 12.7   **(c)** 19.6

2 (a) $\frac{17}{24}$ **(b)** $1\frac{1}{8}$ **(c)** $1\frac{3}{4}$ **(d)** $\frac{11}{20}$ **(e)** $\frac{9}{20}$

3 (a) As f(x) is a probability density function,

$$\int_0^2 (x + ax^3)\,dx = 1 \implies \left[\tfrac{1}{2}x^2 + \tfrac{1}{4}ax^4\right]_0^2 = 1$$

$$\implies \tfrac{1}{2}(4) + \tfrac{1}{4}a(16) = 1 \implies 4a = -1 \implies a = -\tfrac{1}{4}$$

(b) (i) $E(X^2) = \int_0^2 x^2\left(x - \tfrac{1}{4}x^3\right)dx = \tfrac{4}{3}$

(ii) $7\tfrac{2}{3}$

(c) (i) $E\left(\dfrac{1}{X}\right) = \int_0^2 \tfrac{1}{x}\left(x - \tfrac{1}{4}x^3\right)dx = \tfrac{4}{3}$

(ii) 3

4 (a) $\tfrac{1}{36}$

(b) (i) 4   **(ii)** 6   **(iii)** $17\tfrac{4}{5}$

F Variance and standard deviation (p 54)

F1 (a) $E(X^2) = \int_0^2 x^2\left(\tfrac{1}{2}x\right)dx = 2$

(b) $\text{Var}(X) = E(X^2) - [E(X)]^2 = 2 - \left(\tfrac{4}{3}\right)^2 = \tfrac{2}{9}$

F2 $E(X^2) = \tfrac{27}{5}$

$\text{Var}(X) = E(X^2) - [E(X)]^2 = \tfrac{27}{5} - \left(\tfrac{9}{4}\right)^2 = \tfrac{27}{80}$

F3 (a) $\tfrac{3}{2}$

(b) $\tfrac{12}{5}$

(c) $\text{Var}(S) = \tfrac{12}{5} - \left(\tfrac{3}{2}\right)^2 = \tfrac{3}{20}$

(d) $\text{Var}(2S + 5) = 2^2 \times \text{Var}(S) = 4 \times \tfrac{3}{20} = \tfrac{3}{5}$

(e) $\text{Var}\left(\tfrac{1}{3}S - 1\right) = \left(\tfrac{1}{3}\right)^2 \times \text{Var}(S) = \tfrac{1}{9} \times \tfrac{3}{20} = \tfrac{1}{60}$

F4 (a) $\tfrac{8}{15}$

(b) $E(T^2) = \tfrac{1}{3}$

$\text{Var}(T) = \tfrac{1}{3} - \left(\tfrac{8}{15}\right)^2 = \tfrac{11}{225}$

(c) $\text{Var}(4T - 3) = 4^2 \times \text{Var}(T) = 16 \times \tfrac{11}{225} = \tfrac{176}{225}$

(d) $\text{Var}(8 - 3T) = (-3)^2 \times \text{Var}(T) = 9 \times \tfrac{11}{225} = \tfrac{99}{225}$

F5 (a) $\tfrac{4}{3}$

(b) 2

(c) $\text{Var}\left(\dfrac{1}{X}\right) = E\left[\left(\dfrac{1}{X}\right)^2\right] - \left[E\left(\dfrac{1}{X}\right)\right]^2 = 2 - \left(\tfrac{4}{3}\right)^2 = \tfrac{2}{9}$

Exercise F (p 56)

1 (a) $\tfrac{1}{16}$

(b) (i) $2\tfrac{1}{3}$ **(ii)** $6\tfrac{2}{3}$ **(iii)** $1\tfrac{2}{9}$ **(iv)** $4\tfrac{8}{9}$

2 (a) $1\tfrac{1}{6}$ **(b)** $1\tfrac{3}{5}$ **(c)** $\tfrac{43}{180}$ **(d)** $\tfrac{43}{180}$

3 (a) (i) 3   **(ii)** $\tfrac{48}{5}$ **(iii)** $\tfrac{3}{5}$

(b) (i) $\tfrac{3}{8}$ **(ii)** $\tfrac{3}{16}$ **(iii)** $\tfrac{3}{64}$

4 (a) (i) 1.78 (to 3 s.f.)   **(ii)** 1.28 (to 3 s.f.)

(b) (i) 12.8   **(ii)** 275 (to 3 s.f.)

5 (a) $\tfrac{1}{4}$

(b) $f(t) = \tfrac{1}{16}t$ and $f(t) = \tfrac{1}{2} - \tfrac{1}{16}t = \tfrac{1}{16}(8 - t)$

(c) The distribution is symmetrical about $t = 4$ so the expected value will be 4.

(d) $E(T^2) = \int_0^4 t^2\left(\tfrac{1}{16}t\right)dt + \int_4^8 t^2\tfrac{1}{16}(8 - t)\,dt = 18\tfrac{2}{3}$

$\text{Var}(T) = 2\tfrac{2}{3}$

(e) $P\left(4 - \sqrt{\tfrac{8}{3}} \le T \le 4 + \sqrt{\tfrac{8}{3}}\right)$

$= \int_{4-\sqrt{\frac{8}{3}}}^{4}\tfrac{1}{16}t\,dt + \int_{4}^{4+\sqrt{\frac{8}{3}}}\tfrac{1}{16}(8 - t)\,dt = 0.650$

G Rectangular distribution (p 57)

G1 (a) $\tfrac{1}{4}$

(b) $P(2 \le X \le 3.5)$ is the area from $x = 2$ to $x = 3.5$ so $P(2 \le X \le 3.5) = 1.5 \times 0.25 = 0.375$

(c) 4

G2 s.d. $= \sqrt{\text{variance}} = \sqrt{\dfrac{l^2}{12}} = \dfrac{l}{\sqrt{4 \times 3}} = \dfrac{l}{2\sqrt{3}}$

Exercise G (p 58)

1 Mean $= 0$

Variance $= \dfrac{0.6^2}{12} = 0.03$

Standard deviation $= 0.173$ (to 3 s.f.)

2

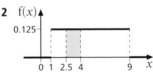

$P(2.5 \le X \le 4)$

$= 0.125 \times 1.5 = 0.1875$

3 (a) $\tfrac{1}{6}$

(b) $\tfrac{1}{6}(4 - 1) = \tfrac{1}{2}$

(c) 4

$E(X^2) = \int_1^7 \tfrac{1}{6}x^2\,dx = \tfrac{1}{6}\left[\tfrac{1}{3}x^3\right]_1^7 = \tfrac{1}{18}(343 - 1) = 19$

$\text{Var}(X) = E(X^2) - [E(X)]^2 = 19 - 4^2 = 3$

(d) (i) 11   **(ii)** 27

4 (a) $(h - 5) \times 0.05 = 1 \implies h = 25$

(b) $2 \times 0.05 = 0.1$

(c) 15

(d) $33\tfrac{1}{3}$

Mixed questions (p 60)

1 (a) $\int_0^2 kx(x-2)^2\,dx = k\int_0^2 (x^3 - 4x^2 + 4x)\,dx$

$= k\left[\frac{1}{4}x^4 - \frac{4}{3}x^3 + 2x^2\right]_0^2 = k\left[\frac{1}{4}(2)^4 - \frac{4}{3}(2)^3 + 2(2)^2 - 0\right]$

$= k(4 - \frac{32}{3} + 8) = \frac{4}{3}k$

$\int_0^2 kx(x-2)^2\,dx = 1 \Rightarrow \frac{4}{3}k = 1 \Rightarrow k = \frac{3}{4}$

(b) $\frac{5}{16}$

(c) $\frac{4}{5}$

2 (a) $\frac{1}{64}$ **(b)** 3.36 (to 3 s.f.)

(c) 3.78 (to 3 s.f.)

3 (a) $\int_0^3 k(t-3)^2\,dt = k\left[\frac{1}{3}(t-3)^3\right]_0^3 = k\left[0 - \frac{1}{3}(-3)^3\right]$

$= 9k$

$\int_0^3 k(t-3)^2\,dt = 1 \Rightarrow 9k = 1 \Rightarrow k = \frac{1}{9}$

(b) 0.0370 (to 3 s.f.)

(c) 0.75 min

(d) $E(T^2) = 0.9$, $\mathrm{Var}(T) = 0.3375$
Standard deviation = 0.581 (to 3 s.f.)

4 (a) f(t)

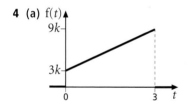

(b) $\frac{1}{18}$

(c) $F(u) = \int_0^u \frac{1}{18}(2t+3)\,dt = \frac{1}{18}\left[t^2 + 3t\right]_0^u$

$= \frac{1}{18}(u^2 + 3u) = \frac{1}{18}u(u+3)$

So $F(t) = \frac{1}{18}t(t+3)$

(d) For the median, m, $F(m) = \frac{1}{2}$

$\Rightarrow \frac{1}{18}m(m+3) = \frac{1}{2} \Rightarrow m^2 + 3m = 9$

$\Rightarrow m^2 + 3m - 9 = 0$

$m = 1.85$

(e) (i) 1.75   **(ii)** 0.6875

    (iii) 4.5   **(iv)** 2.75

(f) (i) 8.775   **(ii)** 66.2 (to 3 s.f.)

    (iii) 18.55   **(iv)** 265 (to 3 s.f.)

5 0.289

6 (a) 1   **(b)** $\frac{1}{2}$

Test yourself (p 61)

1 (a) 0

(b) $P(T < 3) = \int_0^3 \frac{t^2}{18}\,dt = \frac{1}{18}\left[\frac{1}{3}t^3\right]_0^3 = \frac{1}{2}$
So the median is 3 minutes.

(c) $\frac{23}{32}$

(d) $2\frac{23}{24}$ minutes

2 (a) $\frac{1}{5}$

(b) $\frac{4}{5}$

(c) $\frac{1}{2}(2a + 5)$

(d) (i) $\frac{25}{12} = 2\frac{1}{12}$ **(ii)** $\frac{625}{12} = 52\frac{1}{12}$

3 (a) The area for the function is 1, so
$\int_0^4 kx\,dx = k\left[\frac{1}{2}x^2\right]_0^4 = k\left[\frac{1}{2}(16)\right] = 8k = 1 \Rightarrow k = \frac{1}{8}$

(b) $\frac{8}{9}$

(c) $22\frac{2}{9}$

(d) 3.79 (to 3 s.f.)

4 (a) f(x)

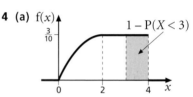

(b) It is easiest to find $P(X > 3)$ and subtract from 1.
$P(X > 3) = 0.3$
So $P(X < 3) = 0.7$

(c) (i) 2.3   **(ii)** 1.03

(d) (i) $\frac{3}{20}(3 + 2\ln 2)$ **(ii)** $\frac{1}{20}(43 + 2\ln 2)$

4 Estimation

A Normal distribution: review

Exercise A (p 63)

1 (a) $Z = \dfrac{X - 10}{2.5}$

(b) (i) 1.6   **(ii)** 0.945 20

(c) (i) 0.132 72   **(ii)** 0.733 34   **(iii)** 0.884 93

(d) (i) 0.8416   **(ii)** 12.104

(e) (i) 14.112 25   **(ii)** 4.112 25

2 0.1118

3 230.5 g (to 1 d.p.)

4 (a) 32   **(b)** 126.8

B Unbiased estimators and estimates: review

Exercise B (p 65)

1 Mean: 11.33, variance: 0.729

2 Mean: 43.8, variance: 195 (to 3 s.f.)

C Sampling distribution: review

Exercise C (p 67)

1 (a) 0.734 01   **(b)** 6.272

2 Because the sample size is greater than 30, by the central limit theorem, the distribution of the sample means will be approximately normally distributed with mean 258.0 g and standard deviation
$\dfrac{11.4}{\sqrt{36}} = 1.9$ g.
$Z = \dfrac{225 - 258}{1.9} = -1.58$ (to 3 s.f.)
$P(\overline{X} > 255) = P(Z > -1.58) = P(Z < 1.58)$
$= 0.943$ (to 3 s.f.)

D Confidence intervals: review

Exercise D (p 69)

1 From 147.99 cm to 162.01 cm

2 From 45.37 mm to 50.63 mm
The sample mean is approximately normally distributed because the sample size is greater than 30.

E Confidence intervals: variance unknown
(p 70)

E1 (a) 14

(b) 2.145

(c) From $28.5 - 2.145\sqrt{\dfrac{18.2}{15}}$ to $28.5 + 2.145\sqrt{\dfrac{18.2}{15}}$, or from 26.1 to 30.9

Exercise E (p 73)

1 (a) 30

(b) 22.29

(c) From $30 - 2.365\sqrt{\dfrac{22.29}{8}}$ to $30 + 2.365\sqrt{\dfrac{22.29}{8}}$, or (26.1, 33.9)

2 (a) (i) 67.36   **(ii)** 39.4 (to 3 s.f.)

(b) From $67.36 - 2.093\sqrt{\dfrac{39.4}{20}}$ to $67.36 + 2.093\sqrt{\dfrac{39.4}{20}}$, or (64.4, 70.3)

(c) Yes, because 64.5 is inside the confidence interval.

3 (a) From $14.5 - 1.796\sqrt{\dfrac{0.194}{12}}$ to $14.5 + 1.796\sqrt{\dfrac{0.194}{12}}$, or (14.3, 14.7)

(b) It is necessary to assume that the resistances are normally distributed.

4 (a) $\mu = 95.5$, $\sigma^2 = 28.2$ (to 3 s.f.)

(b) From $95.5 - 2.160\sqrt{\dfrac{28.2}{14}}$ to $95.5 + 2.160\sqrt{\dfrac{28.2}{14}}$, or (92.4, 98.6)

Test yourself (p 74)

1 (75.66, 76.23) (to 2 d.p.)

2 (a) Mean: 40.5, variance: 1.91 (to 3.s.f.)

(b) (i) (39.34, 41.66) (to 2 d.p.)

(ii) The distances are normally distributed and the eight throws form a random sample.

3 (a) (i) Mean: 3.528, variance: 0.626 (to 3 s.f.)

(ii) (3.085, 3.971) (to 3 d.p.)

(b) 4.1 is outside the 99% confidence interval, which suggests that the mean weight in her hospital is different from that in the region.

5 Hypothesis testing

A Basic ideas of hypothesis testing (p 76)

A1 (a) $\left(\frac{1}{2}\right)^4 = \frac{1}{16}$

(b) $\frac{1}{16}$ is a low probability, indicating that this is an unlikely result if the person has no special ability. However it is not an extremely low probability: more trials would give a more certain result.

A2 12 or more is not convincing evidence, whereas 15 or more is very convincing.

A3 (a) $1 - 0.8998 = 0.1002$, or approximately 10%

(b) 20

B Mean of a normal distribution with known variance (p 78)

B1 (a) $H_1: \mu > 55.2$

(b) $\frac{3.8}{\sqrt{50}} = 0.5374$ (to 4 d.p.)

(c) 1.6449

(d) $z = \dfrac{56.3 - 55.2}{\left(\dfrac{3.8}{\sqrt{50}}\right)} = 2.0469$ (to 4 d.p.)

(e) $z > 1.6449$, so reject H_0 and accept H_1 that the plant treatment does increase the mean weight of the tomatoes.

B2 (a) $H_0: \mu = 94$, $H_1: \mu > 94$

(b) $\frac{3.3}{\sqrt{20}} = 0.7379$ (to 4 d.p.)

(c) 2.3263

(d) $z = \dfrac{95.5 - 94}{\left(\dfrac{3.3}{\sqrt{20}}\right)} = 2.0328$ (to 4 d.p.)

$z < 2.3263$, so accept H_0 that the modification has no effect on the mean lifetime of the batteries.

B3 (a) $H_0: \mu = 94$, $H_1: \mu > 94$

(b) $\frac{3.3}{\sqrt{20}} = 0.7379$ (to 4 d.p.)

(c) 1.6449

(d) $z = \dfrac{95.5 - 94}{\left(\dfrac{3.3}{\sqrt{20}}\right)} = 2.0328$ (to 4 d.p.)

$z > 1.6449$, so reject H_0 and accept H_1 that the modification increases the mean life of the batteries. The conclusions are different because the 5% significance level is a less demanding test.

B4 (a) $Z > 1.6449$

(b) Standard error $= \dfrac{48}{\sqrt{15}} = 12.3935$ (to 4 d.p.)

$\overline{X} > 235 + 1.6449\left(\dfrac{48}{\sqrt{15}}\right)$, from which

$\overline{X} > 255.39$ (to 2 d.p.)

B5 (a) $H_1: \mu \neq 84.0$

(b) $\dfrac{3.2}{\sqrt{20}} = 0.7155$ (to 4 d.p.)

(c) 1.9600

(d) -1.9600; $-1.9600 < Z < 1.9600$

(e) $z = \dfrac{82.4 - 84.0}{\left(\dfrac{3.2}{\sqrt{20}}\right)} = -2.2361$ (to 4 d.p.)

(f) z lies within the lower critical region, so reject H_0, and accept that at the 5% level of significance climatic changes have affected the mean weight of the animals.

Exercise B (p 84)

1 $\bar{x} = 140.7$

$z = \dfrac{140.7 - 125.6}{\left(\dfrac{12.2}{\sqrt{12}}\right)} = 4.2781$ (to 4 d.p.)

The critical value at the 5% level is 1.6449; z is in the critical region, so accept that the seedlings grow taller than average.

2 The acceptance region is $-1.9600 < Z < 1.9600$

$z = \dfrac{5.28 - 5}{\left(\dfrac{0.4}{\sqrt{10}}\right)} = 2.2136$ (to 4 d.p.)

z is in the critical region, so conclude that the mean diameter of the bolts has changed.

3 The acceptance region is $-2.3263 < Z < 2.3263$

$\bar{x} = 50.61$ (to 2 d.p.)

$$z = \frac{50.61 - 50}{\left(\frac{1.2}{\sqrt{11}}\right)} = 1.6834 \text{ (to 4 d.p.)}$$

z is in the acceptance region, so accept the manufacturer's claim that the mean breaking strain of the rope is 50 newtons.

4 The acceptance region is $-1.6449 < Z < 1.6449$.

$\bar{x} = 1.6184$ (to 4 d.p.)

$$z = \frac{1.618\ldots - 1.622}{\left(\frac{0.004}{\sqrt{9}}\right)} = -2.6667 \text{ (to 4 d.p.)}$$

z is outside the acceptance region, so conclude that the sample does not come from source A.

5 $z = \dfrac{1274 - 1250}{\left(\frac{62}{\sqrt{15}}\right)} = 1.4992$ (to 4 d.p.)

At the 5% level of significance the acceptance region is $Z < 1.6449$.

z is within the acceptance region, so reject the claim that the modification has increased the mean lifetime of the bulbs.

6 (a) $\bar{X}$ is normally distributed with mean 30 and standard deviation 0.8050 (to 4 d.p.).

(b) $28.42 < \bar{X} < 31.58$

(c) The mean value is not in the acceptance region, so reject H_0 and conclude that $\mu \neq 30$.

C Mean of a normal distribution with unknown variance (p 85)

C1 (a) $H_0: \mu = 10$, $H_1: \mu > 10$

(b) A one-tailed test

(c) 1.729

(d) 10.09

(e) 0.1167 (to 4 d.p.)

(f) 1.1780 (to 4 d.p.)

(g) This is less than the critical value, so accept H_0 that the mean weight of the sacks is 10 kg.

C2 (a) $H_0: \mu = 3.45$, $H_1: \mu \neq 3.45$

(b) A two-tailed test

(c) -2.064 and 2.064

(d) (i) 3.52   (ii) 0.0267

(iii) 2.142 (to 3 d.p.)

(e) t is in the critical region, so reject the null hypothesis. The evidence points to a change in the mean weight.

Exercise C (p 87)

1 (a) The upper critical value is 1.761 and the lower is -1.761. The acceptance region is $-1.761 < T < 1.761$.

(b) t is outside the acceptance region, so at the 10% level of significance reject H_0 and conclude that the sample is not drawn from a population with mean 133 cm.

2 (a) $H_0: \mu = 16.2$, $H_1: \mu > 16.2$

(b) A one-tailed test

(c) $T > 1.833$

(d) $\bar{x} = 18.2$, $s^2 = 3.5711$ (to 4 d.p.), $t = 3.347$ (to 3 d.p.)

(e) t is in the critical region, so accept the breeder's claim that the dogs are on average heavier.

3 (a) $H_0: \mu = 16.8$, $H_1: \mu \neq 16.8$

(b) $t = -2.844$ and the lower critical value is -2.861, so accept the null hypothesis that the storm has not changed the mean concentration of the chemical.

4 (a) That the 'lifetime' of company B's tyres is normally distributed and that the 'ten typical tyres' form a random sample

(b) $H_0: \mu = 24\,150$, $H_1: \mu > 24\,150$

(c) $t = 1.239$ and the critical value is 1.833, so accept the null hypothesis that the mean life of tyres made by B is equal to the mean life of tyres made by A.

5 $t = 1.940$ and the critical value is 1.699, so reject the null hypothesis and conclude that the rodents living on the island are heavier than average.

D Using a normal approximation

Exercise D (p 90)

Answers are given to three decimal places.

1 (a) $t = -2.009$ and the critical value is -1.699, so accept the alternative hypothesis that the mean number of matches in a box is less than 48.

(b) Because the sample size is sufficiently large, by the central limit theorem the distribution of the sample mean is approximately normal.

2 (a) $t = 1.784$ and the critical value is 2.023, so the difference between the mean ages is not significant at the 5% level.

(b) The critical value is 1.685, so the difference is significant at the 10% level.

3 $t = -2.066$ and the critical value is -2.032, so conclude that the mean number of words per sentence in the second book is not 14.8.

4 $t = -1.871$ and the critical value is -2.023, so accept the null hypothesis that the mean weight of the loaves in the consignment is $0.82\,\text{kg}$.

5 (a) $z = -2.1213$ and, using a two-tailed test, the critical value is -2.3263, so at the 2% level of significance accept the food company's claim that the mean meat content of its pies is $270\,\text{g}$.

(b) $z = -2.1213$ and the critical value is -1.9600, so at the 5% level of significance accept the alternative hypothesis that the mean meat content of the pies is not $270\,\text{g}$.

(c) For a result to be significant at the 2% level, we require the sample mean to differ from the stated mean by a considerable amount so that the probability of this happening as a result of chance in the sample is only 0.02.

For significance at the 5% level, a smaller difference between the sample mean and the standard mean is sufficient.

In the example, the difference lies somewhere between these two. The result is of a kind whose probability is less than 0.05 but not as small as 0.02.

Mixed questions (p 92)

1 $z = \dfrac{9.9 - 10.7}{\sqrt{\left(\dfrac{3.24}{15}\right)}} = -1.7213$ (to 4 d.p.) and the critical value is -1.6449, so reject the null hypothesis and accept the claim that the modification improves the mean fuel economy.

2 $\bar{x} = 52$, $s^2 = 43.824$ (to 3 d.p.), $t = -2.234$ (to 3 d.p.) and the critical value is -2.441. t is in the acceptance region, so reject the department's claim.

3 (a) Normally distributed with mean 100 and standard deviation 3.354 (to 3 d.p.)

(b) One-tailed

(c) 2.0537

(d) Critical value $= 106.89$ (to 2 d.p.); the acceptance region is $\bar{X} < 106.89$.

(e) 107.9 is in the critical region, so the researcher should accept the alternative hypothesis and conclude that the method is biased towards people with higher IQs.

Test yourself (p 93)

1 H_0: $\mu = 56$
H_1: $\mu \neq 56$
Under H_0, $\bar{X}$ is normally distributed with mean 56 and s.d. $\dfrac{4.2}{\sqrt{50}} = 0.5940$
A two-tailed test is required.
The critical value of Z is 1.96.
$z = \dfrac{54.8 - 56}{0.5940} = -2.020$
z is in the critical region, so reject H_0.
The evidence suggests a change in mean.

2 (a) (i) $\bar{X}$ is normally distributed with mean 40 and standard deviation 0.113 (to 3 d.p.).

(ii) 0.05

(b) $(40 - 1.96 \times 0.113, 40 + 1.96 \times 0.113)$
$= (39.78, 40.22)$

(c) A Type II error occurs when H_1 is rejected even though it is true.

3 $\bar{x} = 75.3$, $s^2 = 1.847$ (to 3 d.p.),
$t = 1.629$ (to 3 d.p.)
H_0: $\mu = 74.6$, H_1: $\mu > 74.6$, critical value $= 1.833$
t is in the acceptance region, so the zoologist should accept the null hypothesis that the snakes of that particular species that live in the marshland are not longer than average.

6 Chi-squared tests

B Testing goodness of fit (p 96)

B1 $(15 - 10) + (45 - 50) = 5 + (-5) = 0$

$\sum(O - E) = 0$ for all possible observed frequencies and so it is not useful.

B2 (a) $\sum \dfrac{(O - E)^2}{E} = \dfrac{(15 - 10)^2}{10} + \dfrac{(45 - 50)^2}{50}$

$$= \dfrac{25}{10} + \dfrac{25}{50} = 3$$

(b) No

(c) Accept the null hypothesis that the dice is not biased towards 1.

B3 $\sum \dfrac{(O - E)^2}{E} = \dfrac{(30 - 20)^2}{20} + \dfrac{(34 - 20)^2}{20} + \dfrac{(15 - 20)^2}{20}$

$$+ \dfrac{(17 - 20)^2}{20} + \dfrac{(11 - 20)^2}{20} + \dfrac{(13 - 20)^2}{20}$$

$$= 5 + 9.8 + 1.25 + 0.45 + 4.05 + 2.45$$

$$= 23$$

$23 > 11.07$ so it is in the critical region.
Reject the null hypothesis and conclude the dice is not fair.

B4 (a) 9.488

(b) $\sum \dfrac{(O - E)^2}{E} = \dfrac{(68 - 83.2)^2}{83.2} + \dfrac{(80 - 83.2)^2}{83.2}$

$$+ \dfrac{(77 - 83.2)^2}{83.2} + \dfrac{(93 - 83.2)^2}{83.2} + \dfrac{(98 - 83.2)^2}{83.2}$$

$$= 7.149 \text{ (to 3 d.p.)}$$

(c) $7.149 < 9.488$, so accept H_0. There is insufficient evidence that more books are borrowed on certain days.

Exercise B (p 99)

1 $\sum \dfrac{(O - E)^2}{E} = \dfrac{(20 - 15)^2}{15} + \dfrac{(14 - 15)^2}{15} + \dfrac{(11 - 15)^2}{15}$

$$+ \dfrac{(15 - 15)^2}{15} = 2.8$$

The 95% percentage point of the χ^2-distribution with $v = 3$ is 7.815.
$2.8 < 7.815$, so accept the null hypothesis. There is insufficient evidence that some colours are more common than others.

2 $\sum \dfrac{(O-E)^2}{E} = 4.524$ (to 3 d.p.)

The 95% percentage point of the χ^2-distribution with $v = 5$ is 11.070.

4.524 is less than the critical value, so the results are consistent with the null hypothesis.

3 (a) H_0: RY, WY, RG and WG are in the ratio 9:3:3:1.

H_1: RY, WY, RG and WG are not in the ratio 9:3:3:1.

(b) $\sum \dfrac{(O-E)^2}{E} = 1.724$ (to 3 d.p.)

The critical value with $v = 3$ is 7.815. As 1.724 is less than the critical value, the data supports Mendel's theory.

4 $\sum \dfrac{(O-E)^2}{E} = 3.512$ (to 3 d.p.)

The 90% percentage point of the χ^2-distribution with $v = 4$ is 7.779.

3.512 is less than the critical value, so accept that there is insufficient evidence that the numbers are not the same for every day of the week.

5 $\sum \dfrac{(O-E)^2}{E} = 16.660$ (to 3 d.p.)

The critical value with $v = 3$ is 7.815.

16.660 is greater than the critical value, so accept that the ratio of customers using the four supermarkets has changed.

6 $\sum \dfrac{(O-E)^2}{E} = 5.643$

The critical value with $v = 2$ is 5.991.

There is insufficient evidence, at the 5% level, that the proportions have changed.

Note that in this question (and others of this kind) the observed and expected **numbers**, not the observed and expected **percentages**, must be used for $\dfrac{(O-E)^2}{E}$. The value of this expression is different if percentages are used instead of frequencies, because the numerator involves squaring but the denominator does not.

C Contingency tables (p 101)

C1 (a) $\frac{42}{80}$ out of the 24 country goers would be satisfied, so the expected number of satisfied country goers is $\frac{42}{80} \times 24 = 12.6$

(b) $\frac{38}{80}$ out of 22 seaside goers would be dissatisfied, so the expected number of dissatisfied seaside goers is $\frac{38}{80} \times 22 = 10.45$.

C2 (a) 5.991

(b) $\sum \dfrac{(O-E)^2}{E} = \dfrac{(18-17.85)^2}{17.85} + \dfrac{(16-12.60)^2}{12.60}$

$+ \dfrac{(8-11.55)^2}{11.55} + \dfrac{(16-16.15)^2}{16.15}$

$+ \dfrac{(8-11.40)^2}{11.40} + \dfrac{(14-10.45)^2}{10.45}$

$= 0.001\,26 + 0.917\,46 + 1.091\,13$
$+ 0.001\,39 + 1.014\,04 + 1.205\,98$
(all to 5 d.p.)

$= 4.231$ (to 3 d.p.)

(c) 4.231 is less than the critical value so there is insufficient evidence that customer satisfaction is linked to where customers go for their break.

Exercise C (p 105)

1 Expected frequencies:

	< 1 year	1–2 years	> 2 years
No treatment	29.6	34.8	35.6
Branches cut	26.64	31.32	32.04
Sprayed	17.76	20.88	21.36

$\sum \dfrac{(O-E)^2}{E} = \dfrac{(48-29.6)^2}{29.6} + \dfrac{(32-34.8)^2}{34.8} + \ldots$

$+ \dfrac{(31-21.36)^2}{21.36} = 32.35$

Degrees of freedom $= (3-1)(3-1) = 4$
Critical value $= 9.488$

The value of the χ^2-statistic is greater than 9.488, so reject H_0 and accept that the outcomes are not independent of the treatments.

2 Expected frequencies:

	Strong	Mild
Age under 30	52.79	47.21
Age 30 or over	51.21	45.79

Degrees of freedom $= (2-1)(2-1) = 1$ so use Yates's correction

$$\sum \frac{\left(|O-E|-0.5\right)^2}{E} = \frac{\left(|58-52.79|-0.5\right)^2}{52.79}$$

$$+ \frac{\left(|42-47.21|-0.5\right)^2}{47.21} + \frac{\left(|46-51.21|-0.5\right)}{51.21}$$

$$+ \frac{\left(|51-45.79|-0.5\right)^2}{45.79} = 1.808$$

Critical value $= 6.635$

The value of the χ^2-statistic is less than the critical value, so accept the null hypothesis that there is no association between preference and age.

3 H_0: Male and female students make the same kinds of errors in their written work.
Columns must be combined because two cells have a frequency less than 6.

	Spelling	Punctuation or grammar
Male	34	22
Female	14	20

Expected frequencies:

	Spelling	Punctuation or grammar
Male	29.87	26.13
Female	18.13	15.87

Degrees of freedom $= (2-1)(2-1) = 1$ so use Yates's correction

$$\sum \frac{\left(|O-E|-0.5\right)^2}{E} = \frac{\left(|34-29.87|-0.5\right)^2}{29.87}$$

$$+ \frac{\left(|22-26.13|-0.5\right)^2}{26.13} + \frac{\left(|14-18.13|-0.5\right)^2}{18.13}$$

$$+ \frac{\left(|20-15.87|-0.5\right)^2}{15.87} = 2.503$$

Critical value $= 3.841$

The value of the χ^2-statistic is less than the critical value so accept the hypothesis that males and females make the errors with the same frequency.

Mixed questions (p 106)

1 H_0: The frequency with which prisoners receive mail is not influenced by the length of their stay in prison.

H_1: The frequency with which prisoners receive mail is influenced by the length of their stay in prison.

Expected frequencies:

	Short	Medium	Long
Regular mail	26.14	27.75	18.10
Occasional mail	16.34	17.35	11.31
No mail	22.51	23.90	15.59

$$\sum \frac{(O-E)^2}{E} = 22.93$$

Degrees of freedom $= (3-1)(3-1) = 4$
Critical value $= 13.277$

The χ^2-statistic, 22.93, is greater than the critical value, so reject the null hypothesis. The evidence suggests that there is an association between length of stay and frequency of mail.

2 H_0: There is no link between the schools and the examination grades achieved.

Expected frequencies:

	A	B	C	D
School X	49.8	27.6	23.4	19.2
School Y	116.2	64.4	54.6	44.8

$$\sum \frac{(O-E)^2}{E} = 5.709$$

Degrees of freedom $= (2-1)(4-1) = 3$
Critical value $= 7.815$

The χ^2-statistic, 5.709, is less than the critical value so there is insufficient evidence at the 5% level of significance of an association between school and grade.

3 H_0: There is no association between the predicted and actual temperatures.

Expected frequencies:

		Actual temperature		
		Below	Normal	Above
Predicted temperature	Below	28.39	26.18	18.43
	Normal	29.56	27.25	19.19
	Above	19.06	17.57	12.37

$$\sum \frac{(O-E)^2}{E} = 31.50$$

Degrees of freedom = $(3-1)(3-1) = 4$
Critical value = 13.277

The χ^2-statistic, 31.50, is greater than the critical value so there is evidence of an association between predicted and actual temperatures.

4 Expected values:

	A	B	C	D
Male	15.73	16.72	13.77	12.78
Female	16.27	17.28	14.23	13.22

$$\sum \frac{(O-E)^2}{E} = 12.34$$

Degrees of freedom = $(2-1)(4-1) = 3$
Critical value = 6.251

The χ^2-statistic is 12.34, which is greater than the critical value, so reject the hypothesis that there is no link between gender and preference.

Test yourself (p 107)

1 $\sum \frac{(O-E)^2}{E} = 7.36$

Degrees of freedom = 9
Critical value = 16.919

The χ^2-statistic, 7.36, is less than the critical value so accept the null hypothesis that each of the ten digits is equally likely.

2 H_0: There is no association between test results and school.

Expected frequencies:

	A	B
Pass	113.14	106.86
Fail	30.86	29.14

Degrees of freedom = 1 so use Yates's correction

$$\sum \frac{(O-E)^2}{E} = \frac{(|120-113.14|-0.5)^2}{113.14} + \ldots$$
$$= 3.432 \text{ (to 3 d.p.)}$$

Critical value = 3.841

The χ^2-statistic, 3.432, is less than the critical value, so accept the null hypothesis. The evidence does not suggest an association between test result and school.

3 H_0: There is no link between vehicle speed and the gender of the drivers.

H_1: There is a link between vehicle speed and the gender of the drivers.

Expected frequencies:

	$S \leq 70$	$70 < S \leq 90$	$S > 90$
Male	29.845	41.275	55.88
Female	17.155	23.725	32.12

$$\sum \frac{(O-E)^2}{E} = 25.029 \text{ (to 3 d.p.)}$$

Degrees of freedom = $(2-1)(3-1) = 2$
Critical value = 9.210

The χ^2-statistic, 25.029, is much greater than the critical value, so reject the null hypothesis and accept that there is a strong link between vehicle speed and the gender of the driver.

Index